STONES
TO
Recovery®

For Men

Don't Care
For Care About
I Don't want to
Be A Human
Spirit

STEPPING STONES TO Recovery®

For Men

Experience the miracle of 12 Step Recovery

Edited by Stephen Beal

HAZELDEN®

INFORMATION & EDUCATIONAL SERVICES

Hazelden
Center City, Minnesota 55012-0176
1-800-328-0094
1-651-213-4590 (Fax)
www.hazelden.org

First published 1992 by Glen Abbey Books, Inc.
First published by Hazelden Foundation 1999.
Cover design by Graphiti, Inc., Seattle, Washington

Article No. 44 taken from *The A.A. Grapevine*, March
1962 (© by The A.A. Grapevine, Inc. Reprinted with
permission).

Library of Congress Cataloging-in-Publication Data
Stepping stones to recovery : for men / edited by
Stephen Beal.
      p.   cm.
    ISBN 1-56838-509-9
    1. Substance abuse—Patients—Rehabilitation—
Miscellanea.
    2. Twelve-step programs—Miscellanea.

RC564.S76   1992
362.29'186'081—dc20   92-20195
                              CIP

First Edition
ISBN 1-56838-509-9
Printed in the United States of America

10 9 8

DEDICATED TO
ALL THE GUYS IN THE GROUP

CONTENTS

PREFACE

This book could not have been completed without the participation of Bill Pittman and Todd Weber. They came through with the writing, editing, and publishing skills that ensure the book's appeal to a diversity of recovery needs. Throughout the compilation, many other people helped with their stories, their insights, and their dedication to the 12 Steps.

Once again, the *we* program has produced a *we* book, and we hope that all of you will find reading it as profitable to your program as we found putting it together profitable to ours.

Stephen Beal, Editor

GUIDE TO DAILY READING

January		February		March	
1.	p.80 #44	1.	p.101 #55	1.	p.12 #8
2.	p.211 #114	2.	p.1 #1	2.	p.112 #63
3.	p.6 #4	3.	p.122 #69	3.	p.53 #29
4.	p.103 #56	4.	p.176 #97	4.	p.168 #92
5.	p.175 #96	5.	p.40 #21	5.	p.118 #67
6.	p.34 #18	6.	p.108 #61	6.	p.29 #16
7.	p.134 #76	7.	p.91 #48	7.	p.131 #74
8.	p.53 #29	8.	p.150 #84	8.	p.68 #37
9.	p.163 #90	9.	p.16 #10	9.	p.197 #106
10.	p.96 #52	10.	p.157 #87	10.	p.51 #27
11.	p.21 #12	11.	p.54 #30	11.	p.204 #110
12.	p.106 #59	12.	p.95 #51	12.	p.7 #5
13.	p.147 #82	13.	p.186 #102	13.	p.129 #73
14.	p.50 #26	14.	p.42 #22	14.	p.93 #50
15.	p.133 #75	15.	p.114 #65	15.	p.49 #25
16.	p.73 #39	16.	p.140 #78	16.	p.78 #42
17.	p.154 #86	17.	p.7 #5	17.	p.142 #79
18.	p.9 #6	18.	p.137 #77	18.	p.22 #13
19.	p.217 #116	19.	p.52 #28	19.	p.124 #70
20.	p.59 #32	20.	p.86 #45	20.	p.31 #17
21.	p.91 #49	21.	p.188 #103	21.	p.205 #111
22.	p.99 #54	22.	p.39 #20	22.	p.74 #40
23.	p.15 #26	23.	p.105 #58	23.	p.206 #112
24.	p.198 #107	24.	p.192 #105	24.	p.4 #3
25.	p.199 #108	25.	p.47 #24	25.	p.104 #57
26.	p.66 #35	26.	p.201 #109	26.	p.210 #113
27.	p.190 #104	27.	p.97 #53	27.	p.212 #115
28.	p.113 #64	28.	p.11 #7	28.	p.37 #19
29.	p.2 #2	29.	p.80 #44	29.	p.107 #60
30.	p.180 #99			30.	p.76 #42
31.	p.177 #98			31.	p.9 #6

1. GETTING CAUGHT

When I was using, manageability meant not getting caught. Manageability meant getting by again, keeping the scam going, not letting on, not letting anybody else catch on, not admitting anybody else could catch on, staying away from folks who did catch on. Being cool—or at least looking cool.

Now my life is different. Now I'm out in the open. Now I've admitted I am powerless. Now I've said I need help in living my life.

Now that I am serious about working my program, I should be *willing* to be caught. I should be willing to admit that I could have done better at that job. That I wasn't very pleasant company last night. That I shouldn't have acted out with that other driver. That I should have practiced the Twelve Steps instead of my anger, or my isolation, or my pride.

Who catches me? When I'm really lucky, I catch myself. I apply the Seventh Step (humbly asking that defects be removed) or the Ninth Step (making amends) or the Tenth Step (promptly admitting I am wrong).

Other times people in the program catch me. Something I hear at a meeting will give me a sudden insight into my own behavior. I'll say to myself, "Hey, the jerky thing that guy did? I've done that, too."

Sometimes a sponsor or a fellow member will point out a defect in operation. Sometimes it will be a co-worker. Sometimes it will be a family member or a friend.

But whoever catches me attests to the function of a Higher Power in my life. Whoever catches me shows me I am not alone. When I get "caught," I learn that I am part of a community in action. And in this case the action is helping me grow.

2.   I WAS N.U.T.S.

I got through treatment and got my six-month medallion. Things were O.K. During my seventh month, I really hit a brick wall and felt like using again. I've gotten through that period when I was N.U.T.S. You know, "Not Using The Steps." All I had been doing was being a Two-Stepper. I wasn't using (Step 1); I was going to a lot of meetings; and I was carrying the message (Step 12). I've found out now I'd better learn what the message is first, by working all 12 Steps.

Most of us are used to eating our desserts before dinner is over. We celebrate before we've won. We assume the outcome before the event. The problem with this type of behavior is it takes no account of reality. Things move from beginning to end. The alphabet reads from A to Z. This seems so simple, but it can be tricky for people like you and me who are used to taking shortcuts.

My sponsor has helped me change from being a Two-Stepper to working all the Steps. I had the same sponsor during my first six months and during my seventh month crisis. There's a difference now, because I call my sponsor. Before I just said I had a sponsor, but didn't call him. It's important I put all my effort into every Step. If I do, the outcome will take care of itself. Just like the slogan says, "We are responsible for the effort, not the outcome."

My sponsor told me to read "No Free Ride" in my daily meditation book, *Easy Does It*. I'd like to share it with you:

NO FREE RIDE
The elevator is broken; use the Steps.

—Anonymous

Elevators are easy. We push a button and we go right to the top. The way is fast, quick, and silent. We don't work up a sweat. We don't get out of breath. We can't trip and fall. There is not much time to communicate with anyone else along the way so we don't have to use any effort or thought.

We can daydream as we face the front of the car and stare at the numbers as they change from floor to floor.

Then the elevator breaks and we crash to the ground. Those of us who survive are told to take the Steps to get where we want to go. Our addictions were our elevators out of living. The chemical highs we experienced were just like an elevator ride. Until we crashed.

I will sometimes sweat, stumble, get out of breath in my climb, but I'll take the time to talk with and learn from others who are taking the Steps with me.

3.   FEELING GOOD ABOUT MYSELF

When I first came into the program, I didn't know what I was doing. All I knew was what I *wasn't* doing. I wasn't drinking. I wasn't using drugs. I wasn't leaning on the crutches that had supported me for twenty-six years. Twenty-six years of hiding out from the world and making fun of the world and pretending I was king of the world—all while the world went its own way, far away from me, and I went my way, down to despair and degradation and disgust. Hardly what you'd call a royal progression.

It took me a while in the program to realize that what I wasn't doing—using and abusing—was making me feel better about myself. But here's something strange: after all the years of puffing myself up, constructing largely imaginary successes for myself, the result of feeling better about myself was *not* pride. The result of my improved self-image was not ego celebration. The result of getting to like myself a little was a sense of relief, a very quiet, very steady joy that I was getting rid of the monster, that paranoid self-centered despot at the base of my being who demanded more than anyone could ever provide, family or friends or self or, gosh, even booze or drugs.

I started to take care of myself again. I had the apartment painted. I instigated a birthday party for my stepfather. I got back in touch with old friends. I made new friends, program friends, and some of the fun we had together made me feel like I was back in high school. Back before I started using and abusing, when I could just have fun being alive.

Did I do this for myself? I did not. I just punched the time clock every day: the time clock of meetings and the time clock of not using. I showed up for my life, and a power greater than myself showed me the way. Some days I called the power the Fellowship; some days I called the power God.

But no matter what I called the power I was learning that the power was not me.

What a relief! I no longer had that huge ability to make myself miserable. I was starting to learn the small ways to make myself feel good.

4.   BREAKING THE CIRCLE OF DECEIT

In my using days, I lived my life in fear. I was afraid to face reality so I drank to stay hidden. Then I was afraid not to have enough money to buy my liquid hiding-place so I pummeled myself into going to work. At work I beat myself up with the fear that they'd learn I was a drunk, so I overachieved to prove "them" wrong. Then I dragged myself home exhausted from my fearful posturings and drank to celebrate the real me, the big me, the major me. This was the guy that the working obscured. This was the macho, take-charge, take-this-job-and-shove-it dude who was one day going to put it all together and...and...and...

have another drink.

Having another drink was as far as I ever got with my grandiose schemes, but that was okay, too. In fact, that was great because I never had to test my schemes against reality. I could just sit there attached to my fantasy IV, my gurgling bottle of fraud, and dream away my angers and resentments and frustrations and disappointments in a drunken sunset of self-induced glory.

Then waken to another dawn of despair.

The dreams I dreamed to escape from reality were not real. I was just an average guy. The fears I used as a self-propelling cattle-prod were not real. No one at work suspected I was a drunk; they just thought I was a loud obnoxious hotshot goon. And even that person wasn't real because underneath my take-charge role I was actually a frightened little kid.

These days I get up and face myself as I am. I face the world as it is. In the long run it's much easier to live in reality than it ever was in egocentric dreams. I don't have to figure out how to fool the world again. I don't have to figure out how to fool myself again.

I just am, and I try to make the most of that wonderful privilege.

5. GOD WANTS US TO GET BETTER

God wants us to get better. That's why He extended His grace to us when we admitted we were powerless. He took us in and helped us to accept our program. He showed us the mercy of His ways.

God wants us to keep getting better. That's why we face examples of our powerlessness every day, so that we may learn to turn to God in all our affairs.

God is very much like us. He wants to be loved. He wants to be used. He wants to take part. He wants to be an active force in our lives. He doesn't want to sit around on the sidelines, kicking the turf. He wants to play.

Each one of us represents an opportunity for God. When we have trouble on the job, trouble at home, maybe even trouble in the Fellowship, God is there for us. God is there to help us ease our anger and our heartache and our hurt egos. He is there to catch us when we let go. He is there to provide that Good Orderly Direction when we say, "I can't. You can. Take charge."

Some days it's easier to admit our powerlessness than others. We can always reach out when life bowls us over. But we have to remember to turn to God in the good times, too. When we get the raise, when we finish a difficult job, when that other person suddenly becomes significant in our life—those are the extra special times we have to remember to thank God for pitching in.

No doubt about it. God helps us get over all the hurdles, even success.

6.   THE NEED TO HIT BOTTOM

Why did it have to get so bad before we got help? Why did we have to hurt so much and suffer so much and need so much before we accepted the program? Couldn't we have just enrolled in the program a year or so before our lives became a shambles?

In most cases no. In most cases, God cannot step into our lives until we ask Him in. God can't go to work until we are ready to love Him, and trust Him, with no holds barred. And not because God is standoffish or judgmental. Not at all. God is always ready for us, always ready to accept our love. But only when we come to Him.

Most of us have been supervised at some point in our lives, by parents or sponsors or bosses. What's the difference between Dad asking me to rewire the stereo and me surprising Dad by doing it myself? What's the difference between my sponsor saying I need to do a quiet time and my calling up my sponsor to say, "Hey, there was this great reading in my meditation book this morning and...." What's the difference between my boss telling me that report is due Thursday at noon, no fail, and me coming in Wednesday morning to say, "Here it is, Boss, that report you wanted tomorrow. And listen to this. I think we've got a chance to...."

What's the difference? My enthusiasm for what I have done. My participation in what I have done. My willingness to do what I have done. My joy that it is done. My love for whatever it is I have done because I am connected to it by inspiration and involvement.

If the idea comes from me, I'll accept it. If the idea comes from the outside—no matter how good that idea is—my first impulse will be to fight it. Criticize it. Nitpick it. Search it out for every conceivable flaw. Try to change it and modify it and make it my own. Which it will never be, because it came from the outside.

God knows our characters. He knows we're stubborn. Hard-headed. He knows that if someone tells us that it's Monday, we'll shoot back "Not in Borneo."

Hey—the only chance we've ever had to get better was to come to God on our own, on our knees. And isn't it great? As soon as we get humble, as soon as we honestly ask for help, it feels like we are eight feet tall. Because we have joined forces with a Higher Power, who has been waiting all these years, praying we would come to Him.

7.   CARETAKING

In meetings, we hear "Don't care FOR, care ABOUT." When we care *for* someone, we are letting that person be the focus of our lives. We take over the decisions and responsibilities for that person. We can bond with someone a lot better than with their needs. When we care *about* someone, we are concerned about their journey. We nurture, encourage, and support them on their way.

Many of us have to learn to give up playing the role of caretaker with people. We have been a one-person Humane Society, moving from place to place, picking up stray dogs and cats. We are told that caretaking is an improper response to our need to be accepted.

Whatever the reason we play the role, it is not helpful to continue in recovery. We need to let people care for their own needs. Everyone should have the opportunity to love themselves.

I've learned that caring FOR someone will probably cause the relationship to fail. Caring ABOUT them will allow the relationship and the person to succeed.

8.   HANDLING ANGER

I'd been in the program almost five years but I just couldn't seem to get rid of my anger. You name it, it teed me off. The weather, my job, my girl-friend, most of the sports teams, anyone who dis-agreed with me at meetings, anyone in a restaurant who didn't bring my food right away, any drivers who didn't get out of my way when they saw me coming.

Sounds like I was old and sour, doesn't it? But I was only twenty-eight at the time, a relatively young guy who had many of his best years ahead.

What was my problem? As I say, I'd been in the program five years. But I see now that I had made only a partial entry. I had made a physical surrender in that I was no longer drinking or using drugs. I was clean and I was dry, but I certainly wasn't sober. Not only was I not getting any fun out of life, I was putting a fair degree of misery into life, my own and other people's. Because I hadn't made a spiritual surrender.

I hit my bottom on a Saturday afternoon. Things had been going really bad for almost three weeks. My girlfriend had dumped me. I'd lost a lot of money in a bad investment. My apartment looked terminal. Ditto my car. And now, on a sunny afternoon in April, as I was driving down the street, a bunch of teenagers started taunting me. Leaning from their windows front and back. Making fun of me. My car. My driving.

They're only kids, I told myself. Then I told myself I wanted to kill them. And their car. At the next intersection I screeched to a stop. I grabbed a hammer from the back seat and started getting out of the car. I could almost feel the steam jetting from my ears.

And then I stopped.

"This is the program?" I thought. "This is the program with the motto 'Easy Does It'?"

I never got out of the car. I threw the hammer back in the back seat. I let the teenagers drive away.

Then I drove back to the apartment. Very slowly. When I got there, what I thought I wanted to do was clean the place up. Instead, I just sat down. I sat down in the middle of the mess I wasn't even looking at and I started talking to God. I started asking God for help. I started admitting, out loud, that I needed help. And then, God help me, I cried.

In those days, I didn't usually go to a meeting Saturday night, but that night I did. In fact, I started doing what amounted to a thirty and thirty. I started doing a quiet time every morning. I started talking to my sponsor more. I started talking about what my anger had done to me—and what it had almost done to those kids. I started sharing what a miserable kind of life my failure to make that surrender had led me into, and in the process I found that I was actually making that surrender.

Folks don't call me Smiley yet, but the main thing is, they don't call me dumb.

9.   GOD OR THE GROUP?

When I first came in, I was overjoyed to meet God. This was an introduction that I felt was long overdue. I realized that I had just been pining for God, eager for His company, eager to walk out in the world arm in arm with this Force that had saved me from disaster.

I talked a lot about God at meetings. How I loved Him. How I wanted to serve Him. How close I felt to Him. How much we were going to do together, God and I, now that we were finally friends. My relationship with God seemed to be the most meaningful one I'd ever had, I said, I who had been alone in my pride for so long.

People listened. People thanked me for what I had to say. But I see now that they didn't get enthusiastic. They were polite, but they weren't really buying my message. At least not the way I packaged it. They weren't running around saying, Hey, this guy has really got the program. In fact, they seemed to be waiting for something that I *hadn't* said, something that I *hadn't* done. And I thought getting straight with God was all that mattered.

Well, I can't pinpoint exactly when the change came, but I do know that I started to suspect that it's a lot easier to love God than it is to love people. And I began to be really suspicious of my motivations when I found myself saying that God would understand me, even if "they" didn't. Was I using God the way I had used booze, as a sort of private, selfish turn-on?

Then I started to realize that loving people is a way of loving God. That God gives us each other in order that we may practice what we learn from Him.

Then I started to understand that God uses other people to communicate *to* us. He uses their words— and He also uses their silences. Like the folks with their hands on their chins at those meetings when I kept going on about my relationship with God.

Yes, I see it now. I see what their unenthusiasm had been telling me. That I'd been arrogant. Grandiose. A spiritual braggart. As proud of my sober relationship with God as I'd been proud of my material possessions while I was drinking. The people had been waiting for me to get out of my pride in that elevated relationship with God and come back down to earth with them.

When I stopped making a kind of wall between myself and other people with all my talk about God, I found that I was beginning to develop relationships *with* those people. And, in turn, those relationships led me back to a renewed appreciation of God.

I never have to be alone if only I show love— to God *and* the group. In fact, I have learned that God and the group are usually one.

10.   SEEK UNTIL YOU FIND

When I'd been around the program for a while and seemed to be on solid footing about not drinking, I started a long process of discovering my Higher Power and learning about the spiritual nature of my life. Like a lot of people who come into recovery, I had a true resistance to "God talk," mostly based on my experience in the church I had grown up in, one I rejected as a rebellious young adult.

I also noticed that many of the people who were the loudest and bravest about expressing their new-born belief at meetings were exactly the kind of people that helped me leave the church in the first place.

I tried being tolerant. I certainly learned the difference between religion and spirituality. I knew there was an emptiness in my life that I wanted to fill. My sponsor and I talked about it a lot. We talked about the Third Step, and learning to surrender...even if it was just to the hope and dream of being in touch with a Higher Power. We talked about the Eleventh Step. It was here that my sponsor gave me one of the greatest gifts I've received in recovery.

He told me the story of his struggle with the Eleventh and what his sponsor had him do. He made up little signs from one of those labeling tape guns that had the word "seek" imprinted. He put one on his phone. He put one on his mirror. He put one on the dashboard of his car. He put one on his desk at work. He placed "seek" at all the important places in his life. He wanted to remind himself that the most important part of the Step is seeking, not finding.

That perspective made great sense to me and I started using the same device. I put "seek" everywhere in my life. I sought the spiritual. I sought the connection. I sought to be open and aware. I sought to be non-judgmental. I sought to be giving. I sought a way or path that was right for me.

By placing "seek" in my life that way, I was able to let go of the intuitive dislike and distaste with the "born again" faction. I was able to look in other places and systems. I was able to take a meditation class and learn about yoga. I studied Zen traditions and Sufi prayers. I learned about breath. I found a comfortable way to relate to my Search and my connection with the universe.

I recommend the "seek" method whenever I hear of someone struggling with the Eleventh Step. It is a very good way to learn a new way of seeing and being in the world. It is also a good way to put the rest of the Steps in a philosophical framework that de-mystifies them and allows some questioning and growth. I think the concept of "seek" is very important for men, especially.

It is a way of opening to the struggle for intimacy and contact. By learning to open to a spiritual journey through seeking, we can also learn to open to an intimate journey in relationships. It grounds the experience and makes it less "esoteric," plus it is very practical. I can't say enough for what "seek" has helped me find.

11. THE DOWN-TO-EARTH NATURE OF SPIRITUALITY

If a drinker had asked me, back when I was drinking, what spirituality meant to me, I probably would have made some dumb remark about my glass of scotch. The effect of the spirits on my brain. If a sober person had asked me about spirituality, someone like a teacher or a priest or a civic leader, I would have made an elaborately pious explanation, something like giving away everything I had to the poor and going to live in the desert where I would have only lizards for company.

It would never have occurred to me to say that spirituality was making coffee for a bunch of drunks. I couldn't have imagined explaining spirituality by saying I was going to listen to another guy tell me where he thought he'd gone wrong in life. "What do I have to do with another guy's mistakes?" I would have said. "I am an individual who has got a hell of a lot of his own problems. So come on, don't bother me with someone else's troubles. And for God's sake, give me a drink."

For God's sake these days, ain't no one giving me a drink. For God's sake these days I spend a lot of time every week listening to other people's problems, and other people's solutions. I do this listening in meetings, I do this listening when I get together with my sponsor, I do this listening when I go for coffee with friends. I do this listening when I read the Big Book or the Twelve and Twelve or other recovery literature. I do this listening when I read anything that anybody else has written about getting through this life, and learning from this life, and becoming willing to learn and change and grow.

I do this listening at work (how is Peg dealing with her son today?), I do this listening when I sit down in front of the TV (how do people in sitcoms manage to be friends again after having made such fools of themselves?), I do this listening when I read the paper or a magazine. I do this listening when I am taking part in life.

And that's what spirituality is. For me. Taking part in life. That's what spirituality *has* to be for me. Always being here. Always being present. Always listening in. Always acting in. Always sharing. Always being willing to do all of the above.

I need people. I am a crummy human being when I am alone. I start living in my head instead of in my heart. I start making stuff up instead of living stuff out. I start behaving exactly as I did when I was drinking, thinking I can do everything and thinking I can do nothing, imagining myself alternately God and worm ....

When what I really am is a struggling human being, a man who needs the company of other men and women, who needs to hear what other people have to say, who has to learn how other people get through life, who has to come to an understanding, and an acceptance, of his own human condition.

In the long run, that's the definition of spirituality that works best for me. Accepting life on life's terms. Accepting the beauty of the reality about me. And thanking God, and my fellows, for that reality every day.

12. WORKING ALL THE STEPS

Over the years, these are some of the ways I've heard people "qualify" their program:

Is there such a thing as "partial recovery"? Can we work just a few Steps and leave the rest? Can we just "sort of" do a Fourth Step, like in our minds? Do we really have to write it down as we are instructed? Can we do our Fifth Step with our dog or cat or a favorite tree?

Can we make an amend just in our minds? Can we ask someone to make an amend for us? If a person we can't stand has asked us to be their sponsor, can we say no?

We feel much better about our lives now that we are in recovery, but we really can't do some of these Steps because they're too hard.

After hearing such questions and listening to such declarations, I know the facts are quite simple. Those that didn't work all the Steps DIDN'T make it. Those that do work all the Steps DO make it.

13.   THE PRECIOUS OBJECT

The other day at work, a manager was walking down the hall carrying one of the giveaways she'd ordered for the national sales conference. A custom-crafted version of the company logo, made from china. The manager looked very proud, both of herself and the giveaway, so I congratulated her when we passed.

Back in my office, though, I was smiling to myself. The way she was carrying that china logo—as though it might break any second—reminded me of the way I used to carry myself when I was using. As though I were some very special object. Some exquisite creation that people should feel very privileged to encounter. And very careful about handling.

If not treated with the greatest courtesy and caution I might break. Yes, I might fall apart. I might just disintegrate all over the place, disclosing the awful fact that I was human inside, full of blood and guts and pain. And what I really wanted people to believe was exactly the opposite, that I was perfect through and through, like an artificial creation. Like a logo of myself, instead of the real being.

To keep people from finding out how human I was, I spent a lot of time making sure that nothing would touch me or damage me, that nothing would get through to me and threaten the porcelain perfection in which I appeared to live. I declined a promotion to manager because I didn't want to get involved. That precipitated a break-up with my lover of two years because she'd been hoping we'd get married when I got the promotion.

Fine with me. Her being gone meant I was more perfect than ever. No one to complain about me, or criticize me, or ask me to help with something when I was busy perfecting my perfection with a six-pack or two.

I suppose I should have known something was wrong when the cat ran away, but I just told myself that was even better. Now I didn't have to get home to feed him. I didn't have to bother with his kitty litter. I didn't have to bother, period. Not about anything, or anybody, else. Now there was nothing to bother about but me, me at home alone, wrapped in the protective padding of my headphones and my booze, carrying myself from song to song, and drink to drink, until it was time to carry me to bed.

Six months later I went through treatment, and now it's been three years.

Sure, there are still times when I want to get away. When I don't want to hear, or feel, or know. When I want to run back to my artificial highs and my artificial perfection.

Whenever I feel this way I go to a meeting. Go get myself jostled up with a lot of other people. Go admit how vulnerable I am. Go hear how vulnerable other people are. Go discover how much we all need the blasts of reality we get from the program. Go laugh at myself. Go get broken up a bit to show that what I'm made of is real flesh and real spirit, not some artificial stuff that does not move.

I move today, and very often in the right directions.

14.   SOME THINGS I CAN BE
GRATEFUL FOR TODAY

Today I can be grateful that:

◆ I didn't drink, I didn't use, I didn't overeat, I didn't gamble.

◆ I didn't blame anybody else for the problems that I did encounter.

◆ I overlooked at least two things I could have gotten resentful about. The third one I am letting go of right now.

◆ I dismissed my judgments of other people almost as soon as I made them.

◆ I declined to beat myself up over dumb things I have done in the past.

◆ I refrained from making up bogeymen and putting them in my future.

Other things I can be grateful for:

◆ That I am experiencing my emotions without wanting to run away from them or submerge them in obsessive behavior.

◆ That I am not automatically rejecting any new ideas I encounter.

◆ That I am not managing anybody else's life.

◆   That I am letting God manage my life.
◆   That I am thanking God for doing so.

I can also be grateful that:
◆   I went to a meeting today.
◆   I didn't take anybody's inventory at the
    meeting.
◆   Although I disagreed with some things
    some people said at the meeting, I didn't
    walk out in a rage, or use my comment as
    an opportunity to backtalk, or vow never to
    attend that meeting again.
◆   I gave myself some strokes for the good
    things that I did.
◆   I gave others strokes for the good things
    that they did.
◆   I had some fun.

15.   STEP 6: DROP THE ROCK

Seems there was this group of 12 Step members
taking a boat ride to this island called SERENITY,
and they were truly a happy bunch of people. As the
boat pulled away from the dock, a few on board
noticed James running down the street trying to
catch up with the boat. One said, "Darn, he's

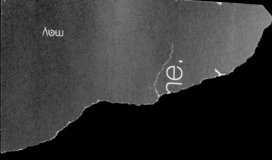

missed the boat." Another said, "Maybe not. Come on, James! Jump in the water! Swim! Swim! You can make it! You can catch up with us!"

So James jumped into the water and started to swim for all he was worth. He swam for quite a while, and then started to sink. The members on board, now all aware that James was struggling, shouted, "Come on, James! Don't give up! Drop the rock!" With that encouragement, James started swimming again, only to start sinking again shortly afterward. He was going under when he heard all those voices shouting to him, "James, drop the rock! Let go, and drop the rock!"

James was vaguely aware of something around his neck, but he couldn't quite figure out what it was. Once more, he gathered his strength and started swimming. He was doing quite well, even gaining a little on the boat, but then he felt this heaviness pulling him under again. He saw all those people on the boat holding out their hands and hollering for him to keep swimming and shouting, "Don't be an idiot, James! Drop the rock!"

Then he understood, when he was going down for the third time. This thing around his neck, *this* was why he kept sinking when he really *wanted* to catch the boat. This thing was the "rock" they were all shouting about: resentments, fear, dishonesty, self-pity, intolerance and anger, just some of the things his "rock" was made of.

"Get rid of the rock," he told himself. "Now! Get rid of it!"

So James managed to stay afloat long enough to untangle a few of the strings holding that rock around his neck, realizing as he did that his load was easing up; and then, with another burst of energy, he Let Go. He tore the other strings off and Dropped the Rock.

Once free of the rock, he was amazed how easy it was to swim, and he soon caught up with the boat. Those on board were cheering for him and applauding and telling him how great he was, and how it was so good having him with them again, and how now we can get on with our boat ride and have a nice time.

James felt great and was just about to indulge in a little rest and relaxation when he glanced back to shore. There, a ways back, he thought he saw something bobbing in the water, so he pointed it out to some others. Sure enough, someone was trying to catch the boat, swimming for dear life but not making much headway. In fact, it looked like they were going under.

James looked around and saw the concern on the faces of the other members. He was the first to lean over the rail and shout, "Hey, friend! Drop the Rock!"

16.   STEP 6: BEING ENTIRELY READY

Just before its discussion of Step Four, the Big Book says: "Our liquor was but a symptom. So we had to get down to causes and conditions." A thorough inventory reveals those causes and conditions; the Fifth Step allows us to share them with God and another human being, and so remove the inner pain they have caused in our past lives.

After finishing my Fifth Step, I discarded the inventory but kept a single page that listed my major character defects. That list would come in handy later.

The first time I read Step Six, I thought it meant I had to arrive at some angelic state of mind in which I would become—and forever remain—"entirely ready" to have God remove all my defects. (I had forgotten that AA promises "spiritual progress rather than spiritual perfection.")

Twelve Steps and Twelve Traditions set me right. It calls Step Six "AA's way of stating the best possible attitude one can take in order to make a beginning on this lifetime job." To me, that means Step Six is not a one-time matter; it stretches over a lifetime of recovery. Even that "best possible attitude" is always just a beginning.

Nearly a year ago, I awoke very early one morning and knew it was time to make that beginning. I took out the list of defects, read it over, and asked myself two questions: "What are you holding on to these things for?" and "What did these things ever do *for* you?" (I may choose to hold on to them for fear of letting go, but holding on to them for years and years led me into alcoholism.) So I got on my knees and recited the Big Book's Step Seven prayer, which asks God's help in replacing our willfulness with His will for us. The "Twelve and Twelve" calls that replacement a "basic ingredient of all humility."

I had gone to Hazelden because I was sick and tired of being sick and tired. When we get active with Step Six, I believe we are sick and tired of being sick—sick and tired of the character defects of which alcoholism is a symptom—sick and tired of their effect, not on our past, but on our present lives.

In this ongoing process, the Program is asking us to go where none of us has ever been before—

into lives of lessened fear, diminished anger, fewer resentments, and genuine self-esteem instead of self-pity. There is a price, however: the willingness to challenge and change patterns of thought, speech, and behavior that may have gone unchallenged for ten, twenty, or thirty years or more.

17.   STEP 6: INWARD AND UPWARD

The first five Steps have supplied the framework for recovery. The Sixth Step begins the active day-to-day solution, removing what blocks us from "our usefulness" to other people, from our Higher Power, and especially (and ultimately) from ourselves.

There are four basic defects that keep us from being "entirely ready." First we consciously decide that we will never give up a specific character defect. Next we blame our defects on others: other people, situations, or institutions. Third, we rationalize. Our capacity to rationalize seems unlimited. Before recovery, we spent years on this one—throwing up barriers against unpleasant realities. Finally, we do the denial thing again: we are totally unaware of our own contribution to our problems.

There's not much use in doing our amends in Steps 8 and 9 if there is no sign of our willingness to change by doing Steps 6 and 7. How many times in active addiction did we say we were sorry without the slightest intent of changing our behavior so we wouldn't have to say we were sorry again? Working Steps 8 and 9 is hollow unless we've begun the active working of the Sixth Step with humility as our guide.

Let's look at the words of Sam Shoemaker to gain some clarity on what the Sixth Step is asking of us. Sam was the benevolent clergyman who ran Calvary Church and Mission where Bill W. (AA's cofounder and primary author of the Big Book) began his recovery. Bill W. credited Shoemaker with passing on to him and the early AAs the "spiritual keys" that make up the Program and the 12 Steps.

Shoemaker wrote about the necessity of making daily surrenders. Yes, the Sixth Step is also about surrendering, just like the Third. But Shoemaker made one point very clear: "We surrender as much of ourselves to as much of God as we understand." In other words, our spiritual progress is based in direct proportion to our dropping the rock. We are very fortunate that all of our defects aren't revealed to us all at once. The way the recovery process works is by gaining daily insight to what we can do in removing what blocks us.

Shoemaker also passed on to the early AAs the idea that "God reveals as much truth as you can live up to." That statement puts us directly on page 164 of the Big Book, where it says, "The answers will come, if our own house is in order." The Sixth Step helps us do that. Some have called the Sixth and Seventh Steps the "forgotten Steps" because they aren't talked about that much. Others have called these Steps the most important.

By working the Sixth Step, we are less likely in recovery to stay stuck in old unproductive, negative behavior patterns. We gain more understanding on how all the Steps, although ordered for a reason, need also to be worked together. *This prevents us from falling into the trap of understanding only just enough of the Program to make us miserable and not enough to make us happy.*

The action of the Sixth and Seventh Steps culminates in letting go—all the grasping and holding to old patterns of behavior, thinking, and feeling that are harmful to our progress in recovery.

For the last word, let's return to Shoemaker, who believed progress in the spiritual life is based on our "looking inward and upward, not outward and downward."

18.   A NEW KIND OF POWER

When I was growing up, I thought it was important to be above other people. I was glad I was the oldest child in the family, glad I was the tallest boy in grammar school, glad I was on the honor list at high school. These advantages allowed me to feel superior to other people and I came to feel that the rest of my life should be a continuation of this elevated pattern. I honestly believed that I would not be happy if I did not have a car that was more luxurious than other peoples' cars, a home that was larger than other peoples' homes, a career that produced more income than other peoples' careers.

When I ended up driving an economy car, living in an efficiency apartment, and working at a modest job, I regarded myself a failure. I was not climbing up the pyramid of power I had constructed in my mind. I was not heading toward any ultimate peak. Instead, I was scurrying around the pyramid's base, like a workman or a drone, seeking just to hold my life together with some work here and some booze there.

Then it was a lot of booze here and a little work there. Then it was pretty much booze all over the place, all over my time, booze and self-pity that I had not scaled the heights I had projected for myself.

Thank God for AA. Thank God for the hands that reached out to me and brought me in and held me close. These hands came out to me from all around, from counselors and medical staff during treatment, from my fellow patients, from the folks with long-time sobriety who came to our unit for meetings, from my aftercare counselors, from all the people that I met at outside meetings as I began to grow in the program. At the end of every meeting I have ever attended, we have all stood up in a circle, joined hands, and said a prayer.

This circle image is one of the most important features of my sobriety. None of the hands that has helped me has come down on me from a superior position of power. All the hands that have helped me have reached out from positions of fellowship around me.

I was not knighted into sobriety. No monarch reached down and whacked me on the shoulder with the flat of a sword and declared, "By the power invested in me, I declare you shall be sober!"

Instead, my fellow alcoholics and users came to me from all around. A friendly, loving group of creatures clustered around me. They told me some stories and showed me some Steps and in that process they were saying, "We're just like you and we have made it. We know that you can make it, too."

These people showed me a path, but it wasn't like the one I constructed for myself while I was growing up and using. The path I have learned in AA does not move up (or down). It moves around. In AA, I am not climbing any pyramid. I am not seeking to attain any position that is superior to anybody else's position.

In the circle of AA, there are no superior positions. We keep going over the Steps again and again. We keep going over the Big Book again and again. We keep telling our stories and hearing our stories and working on our programs together. Again and again. We keep going around the circle.

We're not after power, or honor, or glory for the individual. We're after understanding for the group.

The first word of the program is not I. The first word of the program is We.

And that's what makes it work.

19.   CIRCLES OF LEARNING

I love the circles in the program. I love our tradition of reading through the Steps in Step meetings, and when we finish, reading through the Steps again. Same with the Big Book. When we finish the stories, we start in with the forewords. We never let up on learning who we are and what we need. We never graduate; we just begin again.

I need these circles of learning. I need always to regard myself as a perpetual beginner in the program. After all, I'm no further away from my next drink than anybody else. Insanity could strike at any moment, and I've got to be prepared. I've got to know enough about myself and the defenses I have learned in the program to deal with any emotional fit that could make me drink again.

For me, the four most dangerous fits are:

◆ Rage, those furious gusts of ego justification that tell me I am absolutely right, absolutely wronged, absolutely deserving of justice. (But since life never provides justice the way I think it should, I will provide my own justice. Glug, glug, glug.)

◆ Glee, those giddy gusts of ego fulfillment that tell me it will always be all right, I will

always be on top. (And just to make sure
I stay up there, I'll get stoned.)

◆ Lust, that high-stepping lowlife who tells
me that my satisfaction will never end—if
I just pop that pill, or joint, or jug.

◆ Self-pity, the sob sister of rage, who tells
me I have suffered much too much, much
too long. Poor me, poor me, pour me a
drink.

I can't let these fits get to me again. I've gone
through too much to get clean and sober, and so
have my family and friends, my coworkers, my
fellows in the program. I can't let any of us down
again, most of all me. Because I can't face my using
self again. I can't deal with that jerk. I can't listen
to his bull any more. I can't put up with his tantrums
and his grandiosity. I can't let him lead me around
again by the emotions and the ego. I need....

Well, how about page 449 of the Big Book?
That passage on acceptance. That ought to help me
through my rage. Ditto the feeling sorry for myself.

Lust? There's plenty on that in the Twelve and
Twelve, in Step Four.

As for the good times, the dangerous
everything's-okay times, I always think of a story
in Chapter 3 of the Big Book. It concerns the guy

who recognized early on that drinking was a problem for him. He stopped when he was thirty. Then he had a successful career and retired when he was fifty-five. Surely drinking wouldn't be a problem for him now, he thought. Surely he could control it now. Four years later, after trying every means available to sober up, the guy was dead. Four years of sodden retirement and then a mushy death.

The help I need is always there. I just have to keep coming back to get it—back to the literature, back to the meetings, back to the Fellowship, back to all the circles of learning that keep saving my life.

20. DOING SERVICE

Karl Reiland once said, "In about the same degree as you are helpful, you will be happy." The service work we are called to do in Step Twelve is a result of our spiritual awakening. When most of us thought of service, we thought of restaurant help, chores around the house, washing windows. The thought of service was burdensome if not downright irritating. We probably schemed throughout our lives to do as little service as possible. Every moment we gave to someone else was one less moment we could spend on ourselves. This stands to reason, for we were totally self-centered. Even those of us who "acted as if" we cared normally received much more than we ever gave.

The 12-Step way of life produces "other-centeredness." We, by the grace of God, care less about ourselves and more about our fellows.

When I pass on my recovery, I keep it. This spiritual paradox becomes an all-determining reality for me, that to keep what I have found, I must give it away. Service becomes a way of life.

21.   EASING INTO LOVE

I believe that I have been manipulating love since I first became rational.

Silence is my main tool. When people displease me (when, in most cases, they don't do what I want them to do), I shut up. I withdraw. In *both* voice and movement. They may ask me what is wrong, but I do not wish to discuss the situation. I do not want them to speak. I want them to figure out for themselves what it is that has displeased me. I want them to fix it. I want my world restored to my own terms ASAP, and then I will love my other person as the sun loves the spring. But certainly not as one imperfect human loves another. With tolerance, patience, and understanding.

Usually I know when I have started to care about a person because I start judging what they do. I am getting more serious about them when I start trying to change what they do. And when I start retreating into hurt huffs and sulky snits and deep chill Antarcticas of silence, then it's pretty obvious I am really involved.

Some kind of charm guy, huh? The kind to spend a weekend with, maybe a lifetime? Sure—according to my terms. Because when I am pleased, when my manipulations are working, when I am getting what I want, my charm can be dazzling, my wit supreme, my care and concern for the other person virtually boundless.

Whew! How many aspects of the program does this behavior contradict?

This is not living in the present. I judge others for what they have done in the past and for those infractions I threaten a miserable future.

This behavior is not acceptance.

It represents a refusal to surrender.

It represents unwillingness to change.

It represents the glory of my will and the virtual denial of anybody else's will, including God's.

No doubt about it. Close relationships with other human beings often represent the toughest challenge we face in recovery.

I often get down on my knees and ask God to grant me the grace and the willingness to love without judging. As in so many other aspects of my life, I ask to be freed from the bondage of self.

22.   HOLDING ON TO THE MIRACLE

This program really does it for me. Even when I'm not happy I go to a meeting and I get happy. Not jump-up-and-down happy. Not my-team-won-the-Series happy. I come out of meetings with a quieter happiness. A deeper happiness. The kind of happiness that rests in the conviction that everything is basically okay.

I don't solve all my problems in a flash. But I do gain a fresh perspective on my problems. I understand that they *can't* be solved in an instant. I understand that they will be taken care of in God's good time. All I have to do is keep doing the next right thing. Not everything all at once. Just the one next right thing. As it comes.

Once again, in this process, I am surrendering to a Higher Power. To the *care* of the Higher Power. To the blessed relief of not trying to run the world on my own.

When I was using I nearly killed myself trying to run the world on my own. First I got myself strung out on booze and drugs. Then I got myself strung out on self-will. Then I got myself strung out on the flock of negative emotions that anyone who tries to get it his way twenty-four hours a day is bound to experience.

Resentment, rage, and fear flew back and forth in my consciousness like crows. Big black squawking crows that perched on the strung-out wires of my life crying Big Black Cries, cries like Ruin!, cries like Pain!, cries like Death!

When I think back on what I went through to get into recovery, I see the equivalent of a spiritual swamp, a moral minefield, a path of self-destruction so deep and wide and basically doomed that nothing but a miracle could have saved me.

Every day I sank a little lower into the swamp, set off another explosion in the minefield, told myself another pack of lies to gloss over the horrors that kept going on around me. My assets were stretched to the breaking point. My relationships were stretched to the breaking point. Hope for me was so much a matter of self-deceit that I could not believe in hope any more. All I could believe in was the tricks I employed to hide from reality, and the tricks were getting shopworn as my drunks got longer and flatter and more like the despair I was trying to pretend I did not feel.

If I had had one more drink, one more shot, one more sip, I would have been gone—gone spiritually, gone morally, gone to the physical destruction of cirrhosis, or wet brain, or the final explosive crash, me and a car and a concrete wall.

A miracle did save me.

Now, every day, I thank God for taking care of me, for helping me understand that whatever strength I achieve derives from my surrender to His mercy and His grace.

23.   WORKING THE FOURTH STEP

Okay, who's kidding who? A "fearless and moral inventory"...hah! There is nothing fearless about it, at least for me. It is really more a case of "feel the fear and do it anyway." That is the true essence of courage, anyway, I think.

I've spent my whole life trying to prove I was a man—a "real" man—in some way. Drinking was a part of that. Women were a part of that. Vietnam was a part of that. Sports. The guys. Smoking. The clubs. They all played their part. Yet, for some reason, I never felt whole...complete...I didn't fit in my skin.

In looking back at all the goofy things I tried and did to prove to myself and others who I was, it's a wonder I didn't kill myself. Then, of course, there is all that stuff around trying to prove to Dad that I was really "okay," a man's man: the right job, the right wife, the right house and car, all the different accessories necessary to look okay, successful and prosperous. All the while, I'm being eaten up inside and the only thing holding me together is booze, some dope, and some crazy behavior to let off the pressure every once in awhile.

When all that caught up with me and I was ready to let go of the booze and all that went with it, there wasn't too much of the "good life" left. My marriage ended in bitterness and resentment. The house and kids are hers. The job became a "burden" and I moved on to greener pastures (funny how they didn't pay as well or have as much prestige). I had so much pride—and not much else. It really hurt to face that.

Getting involved in the program seemed to be the best move I made. After a year and a half or so, it became apparent that if I was to keep making progress and moving into a new way of living, I'd have to tackle a Fourth and Fifth Step. I didn't want to plateau, but I had a difficult time getting into that "fearless" inventory. I felt a lot of fear.

I had feelings trapped inside me that I'd never talked to anyone about. I didn't want to write them down. I didn't want to talk about them. I *did* want to stay sober. Eventually, staying sober became more important than my fear of writing about my feelings and the things I'd done.

I'd have to say it was the hardest thing I've ever done: the combination of writing it down, then talking with my sponsor about it. It was also the best thing I've ever done. It really makes a demarcation in my life, *before* the Fourth and Fifth Steps, and *after*. I felt a lot of fear. I did it anyway. I think anyone who says they don't have fear of the Fourth and Fifth Steps are fooling themselves and others. Looking ourselves in the eye may be the toughest thing we've ever done.

But oh! the benefits! To let go of those feelings of shame and remorse and unnamed fears is an unbelievable relief. I finally belonged. I finally felt like a "real" man. I knew who I was and am, and can move forward with that.

So forget "fearless." Feel the fear and do it anyway.

24. FINDING OURSELVES

During my first months in recovery I couldn't stop saying "That's me."

"Yes," I would think, at almost every disclosure about themselves that people at meetings made. "I understand why you did that," I'd tell them afterward. "That's the same kind of nutso thing I used to do."

Hearing these disclosures, I felt like an orphan who has found his family of origin, or like the hero of the song "Country Roads," who comes home to a place he's never been before. I also felt a little like an adventurer who stumbles onto a magic realm, Shangri-La or an ancient city of the Incas. I kept feeling I had found a treasure. These people were just like me.

Sure, I have hard days once in a while. I get angry with the traffic, angry with my boss, angry with the family. But always at the center of my being is the knowledge that I can go away and get calm. I can go away and get calm at a meeting, and

I can go away and get calm in a good quiet time. (A good quiet time is one where I allow myself really to get down into meditation, down out of the I wannas that distinguish my life, down into the universals that unite all our lives. Bad quiet times, by contrast, are those when I just go through the paces, read-my-reading-and-say-my-prayers-and-think-okay-that's-done.)

Finding the people who are just like me at meetings is enabling me to find the spirituality at the center of my being, and this spiritual creature is, I think, the real me. This spiritual creature can do many things that the old material being could not do. He can stay late at work without feeling resentful. He can give up the shortcut home in favor of just driving along. He can say okay when the family proposes doing something at night he had not planned on doing. He doesn't have to go to his special place to feel that he is being fully himself. He finds that he is fully himself when he says yes. When he goes along with the spirit of things, instead of trying to fit the spirit of things into his own self-conditioned ruts.

So what am I saying? That I am most me when I am least concerned with what I want (or what I think I want). That I am happiest when I seize the inspiration of the moment. That I am closest to my fellows, and to God, when I let go.

Walk softly and carry a big stick? Not this guy. I walk softly and carry no stick at all.

25. WINNERS

We came to the Program with different opinions about who were the winners. Some of us thought a fat bank account meant winning. Others looked to how little one had lost before coming into the Program as criteria for winning. There are those who are smart, and others with good jobs. We discover rather quickly that winning has nothing to do with how we appear or what we have.

Winning is about how we *live*. Therefore, we want to watch the men who have had time in the Program. We don't look for just birthday numbers. We watch how the Steps have been and are being worked. We look for the men who exhibit humility, gratitude, and spirituality. The winners are usually the ones involved in service. They understand that to keep what they have, they must give it away. The winners freely share their experience, strength, and hope with all of us.

I want to stick with the winners. If I do, the winners will stick with me.

26.   IT WORKS

Why do 12-Step programs work?

Because we're addicts. Because we are accustomed to doing the same thing again and again. Again and again and again and again. And if that doesn't work, we've got the solution. Yeah—we'll do it again!

We repeated ourselves into states of helplessness and hopelessness and flat-out despair while practicing our addiction, so now it feels right for us to implement our recovery through repeated encounters with spiritual and emotional health. It feels right to keep going back to meetings, to keep going back over the Steps, to keep turning our will and our lives over to a Higher Power, to keep saying, I can't, You can, take over. Please take over. Please, do not let us try to run our lives again.

Our best thinking got us here. We expended years and years of brain power trying to make our addictions work. Trying to justify them. Trying to profit from them. Trying to convince other people that the madness we were putting ourselves through was really very sane.

"Oh yes," says the practicing jay-walker. "This is right for me. This is absolutely perfect." Then he steps in front of the bus and gets both legs broken.

"Oh yes," says the recovering jay-walker. "This is right for me. This is absolutely perfect." Then he climbs on the bus and rides to a meeting. For the third night in a row.

In recovery, we make changes in the negative repetitive patterns of our behavior. As we do, we also change our destination. Now every time we do it again, we're really going somewhere.

27. WHO WE ARE

Now that I'm in recovery I'm straight. I'm also gay. I'm Black, Latino, WASP. I'm a churchgoer and an agnostic, a Catholic and a Jew. I'm a man and I'm a woman. I'm young and old, liberal and conservative, a fan of both leagues.

I have suffered only from alcoholism and I have suffered from multiple addictions. I've been to prison and I've been to Princeton. I come from every corner of the globe, from cornfields and deserts, from cities and villages. I spent my childhood looking at the sea and I spent my childhood looking at a wall.

I'm a family person and a loner, a teacher and a teamster. To get to work I take a subway or a mule. I have been a leader and I have been a buffoon. I have kept my addictions in the closet and I have

fallen on my face in public. I have lost the love of
many and I have gained the love of more. I have
come back from hell.

No matter who I am or what my background is,
I am free. I am privileged. I am proud to be me and
proud to be we, members of a Fellowship who
celebrate the wonder and the joy of being alive.

28.   UNDER THE INFLUENCE OF
THE PROGRAM

Under the influence of the program, we are able
to experience changes in our attitude that we probably would have found impossible when we were
using.

Here are some of the changes I am working on
these days.

- ◆ I try to consider the other person's point of
  view. And the other person's feelings.
- ◆ I try to understand that other people often
  overlook my point of view. And my feelings.
- ◆ I don't declare war when they do.

- ◆ I try to say yes before I say no.
- ◆ Even though I can think of three good
  excuses, I try to say yes before I say no.

◆ Even though it means a change in my plans, I try to say yes before I say no.
◆ Even though I feel I should be granted the Nobel Peace Prize for saying yes, I do so humbly, without fanfare, without calling attention to myself.

◆ I don't try to do everything at once.
◆ Every day I am willing to let go of one thing that I feel I must absolutely do.
◆ Can I remember everything I absolutely had to do yesterday? Did I do those things? Does it matter whether they got done?

◆ Have I laughed at myself today?
◆ Have I let someone else laugh at me?
◆ Have I thanked them for laughing at me?
◆ Okay. Was I at least not rude?

29. LETTING GUILT GO

We could do very little in our lives while our disease ran unchecked. We hurt ourselves more than anyone. We did things we did not mean to do. We put off doing things we were going to do. We offended people we did not mean to offend. We were used to carrying such guilt and regret that it is a wonder more of us didn't take our own lives.

In recovery, we learn how to free ourselves from old guilt. We learn how to make apologies, repay debts, and clean up mistakes through our Steps. We receive an unconditional forgiveness for our past life. We are not unworthy. What we are left with when the guilt is removed is gratitude. We become grateful for a chance to live a good life. We learn we do not have to live with new guilt because we do not have to do things for which we will feel guilty.

In the past, we did the best we could. Now we can do better. We'd rather stand on a mountain top with our arms extended in gratitude than in a hole holding a bucket of guilt.

30.   THE CARE OF GOD

Whenever I doubt that God takes care of us, I think of my west coast trip last fall.

After a business meeting in Portland, I took a week's vacation to get acquainted with California. In a rented Mustang convertible, I drove down the Oregon and California coasts, turned east below San Simeon, and passed through Fresno on my way up to Yosemite. I started this trip on Saturday at noon and by Tuesday evening I was driving down out of Yosemite into the High Sierra.

I stopped for the night in the first town I came to, at the first motel I came to, and after paying for my room, I opened it up and did not like it. I couldn't see the mountains from the window. The hanging lamp was too low. The bathtub was too shallow.

I had been by myself for three and a half days, listening to rock tapes as I drove through some of the most wonderful country I have ever seen. But I had had no one to talk to in all that time.

At the motel I washed up and went out for dinner, to an old hotel up the street where I immediately wished I were staying instead. I was seated in the middle of the dining room—Victorian decor, reminiscent of Granny's house—and all around me there were couples and tables of four. The light from the candle on my table was too faint to read by. I ate half my salad wishing I had bread, then found bread rolled up in the napkin I'd neglected to put in my lap. It was turning out to be that kind of night.

So I finished up my dinner and left the dining room, noticing the bar across the hall. A cozy room, dark and low with soft pools of light. People leaning in from their stools to laugh with the bartender.

I know a slippery place when I see one, so I shook my head and kept walking out. As I crossed the street, which was also the main highway, I noticed a tavern on the other side. Once again, the place looked cozy and welcoming, with soft red and gold lights. It occurred to me that no one in that tavern would know I was an alcoholic.

But I persevered. I decided to buy apples instead. So I walked up the street to the market and the first thing I saw when I entered was a wall full of liquor, mostly pints and half-pints, my old try-ing-to-control-it friends.

Still I persevered. I selected my apples and went to the counter, where the checker was engaged in animated conversation with a friend. Another woman they knew had just left her husband, and the details were pretty interesting. But I was distressed that the checker was trying to force my apples into a bag that was too small.

"I'll do that!" I exclaimed, and did, putting my apples into the proper-sized bag, then stomping out into the night.

I don't know why I crossed the street again, back over to the hotel side, but I did. The only trouble was, so far from the hotel, that side of the street was very dark. No street lamps. No lighted signs. And there ahead of me, on a corner, a group of teenagers were shuffling around in the shadows. Waiting to mug the tourists.

Gripping my bag of apples like a weapon, I stalked bigly and toughly past a group of people who turned out to be all ages, a young couple, a middle-aged couple, an old man. As I passed, the young woman was bending down to the older woman's dog.

"Are you the little alcoholic dog?" she said.

I said, "Are you friends of Bill W.?"

They said, "We're just waiting for the secretary to open up. We meet in the firehouse at eight."

Thank you all. Thank you, Mel and Don and Marilyn and Jack and Sandra and Dale and Jan and Carl and Jerry and Tom. I see you now as clearly as I did that cool September night. I see your faces and your hands as we sit around the conference table in the firehouse, sharing with each other the ways the program works for us.

And thank God too, who is there all the time. I was too dumb to see what I needed that night, but God knew where to send me. Across the highway and up to the market and across the street again and down toward the wicked teens who turned out to be the loving helpful folks I needed.

31.   STEP TEN

Restraint of tongue and pen—boy, I wish I had known that earlier. I don't have too much trouble with promptly making amends and keeping track daily of what's going on in my life, but there sure have been times when I've let my pen take off and say the things I could never say in public.

Step Ten seems to be a practice that one can do forever. Review the day for ways it could have been better—smoother, more open, more accepting, more gracious, more loving—and for ways that it was done well. Clean up those things that shouldn't have been done or said at all. I think this Step is great. It really lets me keep things in perspective.

One thing that helped a lot for me was when my sponsor told me he does a Tenth Step in writing every night. He keeps a journal and incorporates the Tenth Step in his journaling. It made sense to me, so I started doing it too. Boy, is it powerful, sometimes!

Doing a Tenth in writing gives me the chance to go back in time and see my progress. It allows me to see the Sixth and Seventh at work. I can go back six months or three months and look at similar situations, and see how my dealing with them has changed.

I'm still waiting to learn about restraint of the pen, however. It seems that when I write a letter, almost any letter, I can let out all my rage and frustration and bile and bitterness. Something about a letter seems to remove it from me and separate me from the impact. I can't seem to keep from mailing them.

I've written the post office. I've written my Congressman. I've written the mayor. I've written my family. I write whenever I feel there is an injustice that needs to be brought to someone's attention. Soon, I'm hoping to be able to delay mailing these letters for a while, or maybe not mail them at all. It is definitely something to give over in a Sixth and Seventh Step, but so far, I'm not willing.

For now, I'm satisfied with doing a Tenth Step and reviewing my progress in most areas of my life. I'll write you later about the letters.

32. THE FREEDOM TO LOVE

I'm getting married in six months, for the first time at age 48, and what I'm learning from the development of our relationship continually applies to my program. As my fianceé and I work things out, our relationship also reflects my program. I'm learning who I am and what I need at the same time I'm learning that my program works. When I work it.

I've been in the program for seven years, and the main thing I'm learning is that most of my troubles in this relationship stem from the bondage of self.

My mindsets are vigorous, rigorous, and long-standing. I've lived in only two places since I got out of college and I've worked for only one firm in those twenty-five years. At home I know where my things are and I know where my time allotments fall. At the office (I'm an accountant), I have to be careful and responsible in every job I do. Both by temperament and by profession I am a dedicated detail man.

I still can be very stubborn. At my most intransigent, I often resemble an armored tank. I almost literally have to break down my old alcoholic attitudes and habits which have both protected me and walled me off from the world. I continually have to learn to be willing to show myself for who I really am.

This means a lot of changes for me. This means:

◆ I have to be willing to be wrong.
◆ I have to be willing to look silly.
◆ I have to show that I hurt.
◆ I have to learn to ask for help through the bad times, particularly when I cause the bad times myself.
◆ I have to put love first.

In the end, what I'm learning comes down to this: love means never having to say I will not try to practice the program.

33. SABOTAGE

So, you've been sober for a while. Life is pretty good, isn't it? Maybe a little rough at times in the relationship department. Okay, at work it might get a little stressful now and then.

Of course, depression is not a problem, is it? Or anger? Or fear? Then, of course, your finances are always in perfect order, right? Getting sober solved all your problems in one fell swoop—right? You mean it didn't?

There are still some problem areas out there that didn't get handled because we stopped using? How could that be?

I think it could be because alcohol (drugs, gambling, etc.) is just a symptom of our disease. Maybe not even the worst symptom.

Have you ever had a problem getting things done? Just kept putting things off, maybe to the point of not being able to do them at all? Procrastination. Maybe you know it personally.

Or maybe you are the kind of person who gets so wrapped up in making sure each little detail is handled correctly that you miss the big opportunity. Or you aren't sure you could do it perfectly the first time you tried, so why try at all? Perfectionism. Maybe you know it personally.

Maybe you just can't decide. There is so much information available today, so much a person needs to know in order to make an informed choice, maybe it would be better to wait until you get some more knowledge before making a decision. After all, knowledge is power. So, learn a little more before making a decision you might regret. Indecision. Perhaps you know it personally.

These traits we've been discussing are forms of self-sabotage. Some of us have raised these methods of snatching defeat from the jaws of victory to an art form. Maybe it is based in our basic lack of self esteem. Maybe it is based in a weird family background. Maybe it is based in an addictive compulsive/obsessive nature. Whatever it is, many of us let these methods of diminishing our capacity to live fully warp our whole lives. In the program, we need to look at ways of moving past these parts of ourselves that unconsciously block us from living fully and sabotage our efforts to break free.

The first weapon in our arsenal to break the bonds of sabotage is awareness. Become aware of all the ways you sabotage your life. Make a list. Procrastination. Perfectionism. Indecision. Getting sick. Escaping into TV or reading. Overeating. Withdrawing. Judging. Being late. Feeling entitled. The list can go on and on.

How do we become aware of those traits of sabotage that are unconscious? By sabotaging them!

That's right! Sabotage your sabotage. The paradoxical nature of making a conscious choice to sabotage your sabotage makes it possible to bring to a conscious level all the methods and times we might be doing something that is not in our best interests. When you make this decision you will be surprised to see the many traits and habits that are sabotaging your life.

Use this technique to become aware. It doesn't mean the sabotaging behavior will stop. It just means we will become aware of it. Then we can choose. It is something we didn't even have a choice about before. Now we can decide to put it down, let it go, do something else—or just sit.

The next step is to seek the higher level. What is this sabotage trying to teach me? What am I afraid of? What have I got to lose? Who am I trying to protect? All these questions can allow me to gain a new perspective on the sabotage and put it into a new light.

Then, I must take action based on the new perspective. If I have been procrastinating, then it is time to procrastinate my procrastination. I'm going to wait to wait. And, I'll let go of the results. I can control my efforts—I can't control the results. So, I'll let go of doing it perfectly the first time (I'll perfect my imperfection), and give full effort. A little at a time. Each time I can decide to...and slowly, but surely, my sabotage will become awareness and choice.

Who'd have thought that sobriety would lead to this? A chance to move toward my full potential, and to let go of all my methods of wounding and slowing myself.

34. WILLINGNESS

Right from the beginning, right from the time I was a kid, I wanted not to be here. I wanted to be transported out of reality into a place where life was fun. And funny. Where nothing hurt. Where I didn't get disciplined and I didn't have to go to school. Where I had everything my way.

I was born before TV came in, so my first escape was the radio. My favorite show "Dagwood and Blondie" aired on Sunday nights. My pleasure listening to that show was particularly painful because as soon as it was over I had to face the upcoming fact of Monday, that evil monster waiting to chew me up with the rigors of doing things *their* way.

As far as I'm concerned, I was a full-blown alcoholic at age seven. (All that was missing was the booze.) Unable to conquer the twin establishment of family and school, I continued dropping out of the reality I could not control by listening to radio, by reading novels, by going to the movies, by masturbating. Then we got TV and I became a TV freak, sneaking shots from the family liquor cabinet while I stayed up past midnight to watch the very last TV show of Saturday night.

By the time I graduated college I was an alcohol addict. Whenever life got me down, whenever things did not go my way, whenever I wanted to change reality, I dropped out into a bottle. I believed that booze helped me cope, but the truth was otherwise. Exactly otherwise.

Booze helped me *not* to cope, not to pay attention, not to bother. Booze helped me not to take responsibility, not to grow up. For twenty-six drinking years I got my childhood wish: I stayed stuck in the willful self-indulgence where the booze had pickled me.

Now I've been in the program five years. My hair is grey and my outlook is less demanding. I am willing to be wrong; now and then, I am willing to learn. Most of all, most of the time, I am willing to be here. I am willing to find out about the real world whose god I have turned out not to be.

Now I'm taking part in the real God's scheme of things. I am being a true child, and a happy one, when I put my hand in His to go, not my way, but *our* way.

35.   BEING HERE

The most important part of life is being here. It doesn't matter if we're rich. It doesn't matter if we're significant. It doesn't matter if we're trendy. It matters that we do take part.

Being here, taking part—this is the very basis of our program. When we say "Don't drink and go to meetings," or "Don't drug and go to meetings," or "Don't gamble and go to meetings," or "Don't overeat and go to meetings," we are saying "Don't use your obsession as a means of dropping out." We are saying "Stay here by sharing with your fellows."

We are saying, "At least for one hour a day, don't be singular. Be plural."

We are saying, "Don't be I. Be we."

We are saying, "Help us out by letting us help you."

We are saying, "Take the time to allow God to help us all."

36. KING BABY

The first 30 years of my childhood nearly killed me. King Baby attitudes and behavior are a block to recovery. Many of us have carried into our adult lives childish egos and immature attitudes. We won't give up our childlike needs of control or our desire that all our needs be met. An attitude of *I want what I want when I want it,* and motives of power, attention, and instant pleasure have no place in our Program.

Recovery teaches us ways to deal with our scared little child and at the same time allows us to nurture the child within us all. When we act like babies, we think we are the center of the world, and believe that status, fame, money, and power are the most important things in life. When we admitted defeat, we needed to put our childish behavior behind us. We changed from believing in Baby Power to believing in a Higher Power.

We can continue to put away babyish behavior by working on self-discovery, self-acceptance, self-discipline, and self-forgiveness.

37.   WHAT'S REALLY WRONG

Our sickness is not that we abuse substances. Our sickness is that we suffer from character defects that lead us to believe we can fix our lives by using substances. I will feel better, I will feel good, I will feel that I've really got my problems licked, I tell myself, if only ...

I drink some booze...

I snort some coke...

I eat some food.

Then, two or three hours later, or two or three days later, or two or three weeks later, I am totally wasted, totally wrecked, and what will I have fixed? What will be better in my life because I have used? Nothing. Absolutely nothing. For two or three hours, or two or three days, or two or three weeks, I will have had a fantasy that I was in power. Then I'll come to, on the floor or on the street or in the detox center, and how powerful will I be then? How able will I be then to control my life?

We cannot do it on our own. Just because we grow up and have sex lives and jobs and make money and have children does not mean that we know what we're doing. Being old enough to shave every day does not mean that we're in charge, or right, or invincible. Being stronger than our younger brothers and stronger than our old fathers does not mean that we are God.

We are who we are, often jerks, often stubborn fools, often frightened little boys. For most of us, it is not until we are brought to our knees by our substance abuse—by our total inability to control our using—that we finally admit we are not in charge. When we come to the program we finally admit that we need help.

Our inability to ask for help, our insistence on doing it on our own, our unwillingness to share with others—these are the root causes of our using. Instead of asking for the help we need from others, we have used substances that make us feel we do not need that help. We have put ourselves above the common fate of humans—needing each other—and for that violation we have been outcast into the solitary hells of drinking ourselves blind and drugging ourselves goofy and eating ourselves sick.

Once we come to the program we stop kidding ourselves. We stop kidding others. We drop from our shoulders the intolerable, impossible weight of running the world on our own. Here in the program we get down to right size, and right habits, and it's the most amazing thing in the world—because now we're in the world, the real world—but most things aren't as bad as we made them out to be. Most people aren't as bad as we made them out to be.

Sure, there is suffering, there is misery, there is injustice. But there is also love, tolerance, and understanding. There are opportunities to relieve suffering and misery, opportunities to serve justice. If we are willing to work with our fellow humans. If we are willing to be "a friend among friends, to be a worker among workers, to be a useful member of society."

If we are willing to put our pride and our self-centeredness in the background and work with our fellows for change, there is nothing we can't do. In time. With love. And trust.

38.   THE POISON TREE

> I was angry with my friend:
> I told my wrath, my wrath did end.
> I was angry with my foe:
> I told it not, my wrath did grow.
> — from "A Poison Tree" by William Blake

Resentment works like a poison in my life. When I give way to resentment, its poison seems to spread through my whole being, just as water taken in through roots spreads upward through a tree. My body is numbed by the poison of resentment, my mind is numbed, my whole being is concentrated on the terrible wrong I believe that I have suffered and my resulting "righteous" anger. If I were a real tree I would turn from green to black and just start rotting.

Unless, that is, I act immediately to dispel the poison of resentment. This I do by talking over my resentment with the person who aroused it. Just as

Blake says, I treat the person who angered me as a friend, not a foe. I indicate that our relationship is important to me and that I don't want it to suffer because of something said or done which I may well be blowing out of proportion.

Program principles advise us to talk our problems over with sponsors or in meetings, but when it comes to resentments, this habit of ours can often represent a cop-out. The longer I share my resentment with my sponsor or the group, the more that sharing can allow my resentment to grow and fester.

Sure, the "recovery me" seems to be getting the resentment out by discussing it. But the "user me" can still be holding on to the resentment inside. Sure, I say as I leave the meeting, I'll call that guy right now. As soon as I get home, I say. Well, after the game. Unless it goes on too long. So I'd better wait till tomorrow.

Which is much too late when we're suffering from the deadly viper's bite of resentment. Open up the wound and squeeze the poison out. Right away.

We have to give ourselves the opportunity to heal. Otherwise we face the terrible possibility of turning black with our resentment, and getting numb, and rotting away. Which sounds a lot like using to me.

39. LEARNING TRUST

Our entire Program rests upon the principle of mutual trust. We trust our Higher Power, we trust the Program, and we trust each other.

When we were using, we trusted no one. We lied about everything, even the smallest thing, so how could we trust what anyone else told us? Cheating was a way of life. Finding reasons for our actions kept us busy rationalizing away our lives.

So how could we trust anyone? How could we trust ourselves? We couldn't even trust ourselves to keep track of our lies. They were so big and so many and so confusing that we just drowned our denial in chemicals. Then it didn't matter any more.

The only thing we thought we could trust was our addiction. When we discovered it was the biggest lie of all, we lost trust in everything. We had nowhere to go. And that was the greatest day of our lives.

We've put our trust in the Program, the Steps, our sponsor, our group, and our Higher Power, and, little by little, day by day, we are learning to trust again.

40. MY DAUGHTER TALKS TO ME AGAIN!

The other night I was watching TV on the couch when my daughter came in. She's fifteen. "Is it any good?" she asked. "Okay," I said—and then it happened. She sat down beside me, right beside me, just the way she used to do. She snuggled up against me till I raised my arm and put it around her shoulders. I don't want to sound like a corny greeting card, but I will say I had trouble seeing the screen for a while.

It's been three years since my daughter sat like that with me. First I told myself she stopped because she was getting too old to snuggle up to Dad. Too old to play the kid role any more.

Then I told myself she wasn't coming around because she had too much to do. Homework and after-school clubs. Phone calls. Hairdos.

Then I told myself she didn't come around because she had boyfriends. She didn't want to sit with me the way she was sitting with her dates.

At least I assumed that was the way she was sitting with her dates. I didn't really know much about her life because she wasn't talking to me any more. Not the way we used to talk before... well, before I started drinking so much, but, Hey, I told myself, the kid is just too immature to understand the pressures that her Dad has to cope with every day.

Sure, guy. My daughter understood completely the pressures that I had to cope with. My pressures were called Manhattans and I drank five or six every night. Two before dinner, the rest while I watched TV. And started shouting at the set and anyone who happened by. Until I stumbled up to bed or passed out on the couch or ....

Well, they found me on the bathroom floor one morning.

Another morning they found me in the yard.

The morning they couldn't find me, the police did. I was passed out in the playground of the school. The grammar school that my daughter had graduated from and my son was still attending.

I'm still working on my son. He's still frightened of me. Still wary. Still unwilling to trust.

But I'll tell you this. My daughter coming in to sit with me the other night made me know that I'll do anything I have to do to get my whole family back again.

Boy, it's good to feel like my daughter's father again. Instead of like her child.

41.   THE YETS

Nothing is so bad that relapse won't make it worse. The stories we hear in meetings often shock us. It seems hard to believe that some members could have harmed themselves in such ways. We hear about arrests, bankruptcies, loss of family and home, lost jobs, violence, jail, physical injury—the list goes on. Most of us said to ourselves, "I never was that bad. Maybe I don't really belong here."

Our sponsors and fellow members quickly straightened us out. We were *comparing* our histories with other members. We were told to *identify* with the stories, not compare. Some of us had been lucky that worse things hadn't happened to us while we were using. We were reminded those things hadn't happened to us "yet." If we relapsed, the "yets" were waiting.

Today we remember to identify, not compare. We don't want to relapse and go through THE YETS.

42.   I QUIT GOING TO MEETINGS

I used to hear people say there was no graduation from AA and I was determined to prove them wrong. They said AA was a Way of Life and alcoholics kept going to meetings to learn how to live. My compulsion to drink was gone and I thought I knew how to live. I didn't think I needed meetings any more.

So I quit going and after a while I quit praying. Self came in with all its arrogance and started running my life—and everyone knows how well that went. When I started hurting, I wouldn't tell anyone—they might have suggested I go to a meeting and then my argument about not needing meetings would become invalid. I just withdrew, instead—licked my wounds—took a tranquilizer or smoked a little pot. Oh, I didn't drink but I sure was sick. I remember that things got real rough a couple of times and I asked God for help. He helped me just like He always had. But as soon as things were running smoothly again, I forgot about God and took the director's chair again. And just like always, the actors wouldn't do what I wanted them to do and I got angry and resentful and fearful. And life became unmanageable again. I was financially, emotionally, and spiritually bankrupt and I wasn't even drinking.

I hit bottom—again. And I finally understood that "alcohol was only a symptom" of my illness.

I went back to meetings and learned that I knew nothing— that I was only a baby in the program. But I began to ask for help, listened, and shared with others. I rejoined a group and made new friends and renewed old friendships.

Now AA is a school for me and I don't want to graduate. I want to keep on learning the things I need to live a reasonably contented life—one day at a time. I might be in AA kindergarten now; I'm not sure. I know I have to keep this program real simple—just don't drink, don't use, and go to meetings. Who needs meetings? I know I do! How about you?

43.   SLIPPERY PLACES

Here's a place to stay away from. It's a gloomy place, filled with dreams that have not come true, love that has gone sour, friendships that have fizzled, jobs that have deteriorated. Here people are out to get you, to bring you down and make you suffer. Here every car's a lemon, every house on the verge of collapse. Children go wrong here, accept rides from strangers or start using when they're seven. All the appliances are broken here, and everybody's angry. The food's rotten and the air is foul. Flowers die. Dogs howl. The sky is black at noon.

Here's another place to stay away from. It looks like the set from a technicolor musical. Gorgeous women in not many clothes keep descending a staircase. To the right there's an Olympic-sized swimming pool, to the left a Rolls Royce, and in between a man at a mahogany desk is packing a briefcase with gold bullion and securities while he chats on his hotline with the Commissioner of Baseball, who has called him for advice.

Where are these places? In my mind. I create these places, these pure-crap or pure-gold fantasies, when I'm not living in the now, when I am far away from the program and the rational advice for daily living it provides me.

I'm isolating at such times, trying to figure life out, trying to solve my problems on my own. Through these private creations, I project myself into such misery or such glory that I need something—anything—to bring me back to earth. I need not to be in my head, not to believe the nonsense I am telling me.

It used to be when I got in these moods I would use. Now, if I'm lucky, or I'm wise, or I'm just really tired of my bull, I go to a meeting. Call my sponsor or a buddy. Talk out where I really am, what I'm really worried about. Find out what I'm hiding from. Become a human being again, a resident of this earth, not of my headtrip fantasylands.

44.   WHAT IS ACCEPTANCE?
By Bill W.

One way to get at the meaning of the principle of acceptance is to meditate upon it in the context of AA's much used prayer, "God grant me the serenity to accept the things I cannot change, courage to change the things I can, and the wisdom to know the difference."

Essentially this is to ask for the resources of Grace by which we may make spiritual progress under all conditions. Greatly emphasized in this wonderful prayer is a need for the kind of wisdom that discriminates between the possible and the impossible. We shall also see that life's formidable array of pains and problems will require many different degrees of acceptance as we try to apply this valued principle.

Sometimes we have to find the right kind of acceptance for each day. Sometimes we need to develop acceptance for what may come to pass tomorrow, and yet again we shall have to accept a condition that may never change. Then, too, there frequently has to be right and realistic acceptance of grievous flaws within ourselves and serious faults within those about us—defects that may not be fully remedied for years, if ever.

All of us will encounter failures, some retrievable and some not. We shall often meet with defeat—sometimes by accident, sometimes self-inflicted, and at still other times dealt to us by the injustice and violence of other people. Most of us will meet up with some degree of worldly success, and here the problem of the right kind of acceptance will be really difficult. Then there will be illness and death. How indeed shall we be able to accept all these?

It is always worthwhile to consider how grossly that good word acceptance can be misused. It can be warped to justify nearly every brand of weakness, nonsense, and folly. For instance, we can "accept" failure as a chronic condition, forever without profit or remedy. We can "accept" worldly success pridefully, as something wholly of our own making. We can also "accept" illness and death as certain evidence of a hostile and godless universe. With these twistings of acceptance, we AAs have had vast experience. Hence we constantly try to remind ourselves that these perversions of acceptance are just gimmicks for excuse-making: a losing game at which we are, or at least have been, the world's champions.

This is why we treasure our "Serenity Prayer" so much. It brings a new light to us that can dissipate our old-time and nearly fatal habit of fooling ourselves. In the radiance of this prayer we see that defeat, rightly accepted, need be no disaster. We know that we do not have to run away, nor ought we again try to overcome adversity by still another bull-dozing power drive that can only push up obstacles before us faster than they can be taken down.

On entering AA, we become the beneficiaries of a very different experience. Our new way of staying sober is literally founded upon the proposition that "Of ourselves, we are nothing, the Father doeth the works." In Steps One and Two of our recovery program these ideas are specifically spelled out: "We admitted that we were powerless over alcohol ... that our lives had become unmanageable"— "Came to believe that a power greater than ourselves could restore us to sanity." We couldn't lick alcohol with our own remaining resources and so we accepted the further fact that dependence upon a Higher Power (if only our AA group) could do this

hitherto impossible job. The moment we were able
to fully accept these facts, our release from the
alcohol compulsion had begun. For most of us this
pair of acceptances had required a lot of exertion to
achieve. Our whole treasured philosophy of self-
sufficiency had to be cast aside. This had not been
done with old-fashioned will power; it was instead
a matter of developing the willingness to accept
these new facts of living. We neither ran nor
fought. But accept we did. And then we were free.
There had been no irretrievable disaster.

This kind of acceptance and faith is capable of
producing 100 percent sobriety. In fact it usually
does; and it must, else we could have no life at all.
But the moment we carry these attitudes into our
emotional problems, we find that only relative
results are possible. Nobody can, for example,
become completely free from fear, anger, and pride.
Hence in this life we shall attain nothing like perfect
humility and love. So we shall have to settle,
respecting most of our problems, for a very gradual
progress, punctuated sometimes by heavy setbacks.
Our old-time attitudes of "all or nothing" will have
to be abandoned.

Therefore our very first problem is to accept
our present circumstances as they are, ourselves as

we are, and the people about us as they are. This is
to adopt a realistic humility without which no
genuine advance can even begin. Again and again,
we shall need to return to that unflattering point of
departure. This is an exercise in acceptance that we
can profitably practice every day of our lives.
Provided we strenuously avoid turning these realistic surveys of the facts of life into unrealistic alibis
for apathy or defeatism, they can be the sure foundation upon which increased emotional health and
therefore spiritual progress can be built. At least
this seems to be my own experience.

Another exercise that I practice is to try for a
full inventory of my blessings and then for a right
acceptance of the many gifts that are mine—both
temporal and spiritual. Here I try to achieve a state
of joyful gratitude. When such a brand of gratitude
is repeatedly affirmed and pondered, it can finally
displace the natural tendency to congratulate myself on whatever progress I may have been enabled
to make in some areas of living. I try hard to hold
fast to the truth that a full and thankful heart cannot
entertain great conceits. When brimming with gratitude, one's heartbeat must surely result in outgoing
love, the finest emotion that we can ever know.

In times of very rough going, the grateful acceptance of my blessings, oft repeated, can also bring me some of the serenity of which our AA prayer speaks. Whenever I fall under acute pressures I lengthen my daily walks and slowly repeat our Serenity Prayer in rhythm to my steps and breathing. If I feel that my pain has in part been occasioned by others, I try to repeat, "God grant me the serenity to love their best, and never fear their worst." This benign healing process of repetition, sometimes necessary to persist with for days, has seldom failed to restore me to at least a workable emotional balance and perspective.

Another helpful step is to steadfastly affirm the understanding that pain can bring. Indeed pain is one of our greatest teachers. Though I still find it difficult to accept today's pain and anxiety with any great degree of serenity—as those more advanced in the spiritual life seem able to do—I can, if I try hard, give thanks for present pain nevertheless. I find the willingness to do this when I contemplate the lessons learned from past suffering—lessons which have led to the blessings I now enjoy. I can remember, if I insist, how the agonies of alcoholism, the pain of rebellion and thwarted pride, have often led me to God's Grace, and on to a new freedom. So, as I walk along, I repeat still other phrases such as these, "Pain is the touchstone of progress" ... "Fear no evil" ... "This, too, will pass"..."This experience can be turned to benefit." These fragments of prayer bring far more than mere comfort. They keep me on the track of right acceptance; they break up my compulsive themes of guilt, depression, rebellion, and pride; and sometimes they endow me with the courage to change the things I can, and the wisdom to know the difference.

To those who never have given these potent exercises in acceptance a real workout I recommend them highly the next time the heat is on. Or, for that matter, at any time!

45. PRAYER AND MEDITATION

We're told that trying to pray *is* praying. "Oh, God, help me! If you get me out of this mess, I'll never screw up again." This was our favorite prayer before we entered the Program. We were always bargaining with God.

We have learned new prayers and a new way to talk and listen to our Higher Power. We are seeking God's will for us. Many of us had to learn *how* to pray. We began with very simple prayers: "God, help me know Your will for me." "Thank you, God, for helping me today."

We learn that prayer helps us with our overdependence on people, places, and things by giving us the insight and strength to rearrange our priorities. Prayer doesn't change God, but it changes those who pray.

Today in our prayers, we seek our Higher Power's will for us. We no longer bargain with God.

Prayer is seeking answers and direction in life. Meditation is listening for answers from a Higher Power and developing the faith within us to accept those answers. Reflection is finding ways to change the answers we get from prayer and meditation into *action*.

Reflection is understanding how to use the Twelve Steps. It is not snap judgment. It asks us to think of the pros and cons of our possible choices and to understand what directions we will take to give us the best results.

The progress of spirituality from prayer to meditation to reflection is active, not passive. It is taking part in the joy of putting the results of prayer and meditation into action.

We have learned through times of quiet reflection to work into our lives the answers our Higher Power has given us as a result of our prayer and meditation.

46.   I DON'T KNOW BETTER ANYMORE

"Don't drink, go to meetings, and change your whole life around."

That's what they told me when I first came into the program, and I said Sure, the way I used to respond to my mother when she asked if I had my scarf on.

"Sure, Mom," I called as I ran out the door looking cool. Too cool. Two days later I would be in bed and Mom would be looking righteous as she plugged in the vaporizer.

Coming into the program is a lot like growing up all over again. Only this time we start to listen to the oldtimers (even when they're younger than we). This time we try to follow what they say. Sometimes, before we make our first move, we even consult with others about the best way to proceed.

In the program we are becoming teachable, and reachable, and willing to learn, and this is a revolutionary change for me. This is the beginning of humility, accepting that I cannot run my life on my own.

Why did I fight it for so long? What did I produce with my willfulness and my stubbornness, with my insistence on My Way?

◆ I produced Disaster and tried to call it Cunning.

◆ I produced Suffering and tried to call it Joy.

◆ I produced a Negative Outlook and tried to call it Wisdom.

◆ I produced a Self-Absorbed Individual and tried to call him God.

◆ I produced a Jerk.

Now, with God's help, and the program's, and my own (yes, I'm becoming a person I can trust again), I am going to school every day. My school is called meetings and I always sit in the front row. I take mental notes. I don't take others' inventory. I respect the members of the Fellowship. I do what I am asked to do.

And yes, Mom. I wear a scarf when it's cold.

47.   JEOPARDY DAYS

Here's a prayer for those days when we're in danger of doing something to mess up our programs. Not use. Just do something that will make us mistrust ourselves and forget the Good Orderly Direction we have learned from the program.

Please, don't let me believe what I tell myself.

Please, don't let me beat up on me, sending myself to the corner for every misdeed I can remember since I got out of diapers.

Please, don't let me indulge myself, sending myself to the using-substitute places I have found, the ice-cream bar, the pizza parlor, the video shop, the adult book store.

Please, let me live in the now, accepting the pain of the present moment as a sign of growth, the thrusting of a new green shoot through the winter of my mind.

Please, let me call a friend. Let me drop my macho poses and say I hurt. Let me say why I hurt. Let me be willing to look dumb or weak or confused.

Please, let me listen. Let me be willing to accept a new idea. Let me go to a different meeting. Talk to different people. Get home at a different time.

Please, let me be a free man in a free world. Let me stop attaching myself to old bondages or unworthy bondages. Most of all....

Please, keep me free of the bondage of self.

48. PROMPT ADMISSION

If we happened to be a certain NASA scientist, we would know all about prompt admissions. A few years ago, when the *Voyager* spacecraft was sent into space to explore the planets of our solar system, something happened shortly after liftoff. One of the scientists noticed the path of the rocket was off by one ten-thousandth of a degree. It was a very small mistake, but unless the mistake was corrected early, it would multiply itself many times over.

Instead of hitting a target one billion miles away, the craft would miss the mark and the mission would fail. The mistake was corrected, and success was assured.

So it is with our daily inventory. We take prompt and immediate action so we can stay on target. Our target is our conscious contact with God.

When I stray off course, even slightly, I take prompt action to right myself. What appears at the moment to be a minor wrong can quickly grow and jeopardize my recovery.

49. REASONS TO LIVE

Yesterday at my home group, a guy brought in a note he found in his desk while he was doing his taxes. The note was almost twenty years old. He had a hard time reading it because he wrote it after he'd been drinking. A lot of the words were squished and the lines were wavy. But the gist of the note, addressed to his wife, was that he was a worthless drunk who had no right to live, who had no friends, and she would be a whole lot better off when he was gone.

The first guy to comment after the reading of this note told about a suicide attempt he made while he was drinking. First he wrote a long profound note to the world explaining why he could not participate in the world any more. Then he dug out the vacuum cleaner hose and took it out to the driveway to connect to the tailpipe. Son of a gun! He'd forgotten that the tailpipe had fallen off the car. So he climbed in the back seat and passed out till morning.

The next guy to comment said he'd never thought of committing suicide. Then he paused. "On the other hand," he said, "I didn't care about anything when I was using. I was always acting out a death wish. I drank like hell. I drugged like hell. I fought like hell. And the way I rode my motor-cycle...." He shook his head. "There must have been *someone* watching over me."

Here we are, God, all Your children saying thank you for keeping us safe from ourselves. Safe from the dangers we courted to look like real men. Safe from the rages we cultivated to hide our fear. Safe from the strutting and the posturing to look successful when most of what we touched turned to shame and failure. Safe from bolstering our false egos by abusing every substance we could find. Safe from the monsters we let out when we used.

In recovery we have our first real chance to act like heroes. And we're not doing any killing, any damage, any dangerous stuff to ourselves or others. We're no longer using weapons; now we're using instruments of healing. Through willingness and honesty, through action and trust, we are learning simply and gently to put the bad guys—our old using selves—to rest.

50. BEWARE OF THE SOBRIETY MASK

The question often arises in AA circles as to why "John Doe" got drunk after five years of sobriety. Sometimes the story continues: "He was so active in 'service work,' he was at all the AA functions, he seemed to have it all together." The list goes on and on.

I have studied this question and through my own experience have come up with an answer. Not being honest, not fully sharing: those are the reasons we drink again.

Most of us seem to agree that we hid behind a mask before we came to AA. But since coming to AA many of us have formed another mask. The dreaded "sobriety mask." This mask is cunning, baffling, and powerful. While we are behind this mask we deceive others into believing that we "have it all together." But this is where the real danger lies...we also deceive ourselves into believing the same thing.

What is the solution? One thing this false image can't live with, is truth. I find it helpful to ask myself, "When was the last time I shared what was really going on inside me, in my inner-most world, with another person or with my home group?"

You know, the Big Book says we should share our experience, strength, and hope. But, when I'm stuck behind my mask, I only share my opinions, attitudes, and advice. It's safer...or is it?

51. SATIRE, LUST, AND REBELLION

I recently read an article by a middle-aged man whose son came home for vacation. The son, he said, was concerned with the things that most teenagers are concerned with: satire, lust, and rebellion.

Oops, I said when I read this. Some unknown guy had just nailed me where I used to live. I was 31 when I came into the program, and among the traits I prized most in myself were my ability to make fun of things, my sexual adventuring, and my intolerance of authority. If I didn't mock it, screw it, or give the finger to it, I felt I was somehow not a real man. And I wasn't any Hell's Angel. I wasn't a rocker or a hippie or a punked-out freak. I was a guy in a button-down collar who drove an average car and paid his rent on time.

But there was in me a fierce defiance that seemed to exist only for its own negative sake. I wanted to make fun of things because I wanted to feel superior to them, and I wanted to fool around because I wanted to feel good without getting involved, and I wanted not to go along with practically any idea or system that anybody else believed in because I wanted to be My Own Master, no matter what. I was like a bright kid in high school, a real sophomore, who knows the answer to *everything* just so long as he doesn't have to be responsible for *anything*. I was an elderly teenager.

That's why my satires never worked: I could make fun of the surface but I did not understand the basics beneath. That's why sex was never enough: I never allowed it to develop into a relationship. That's why my rebellions were hollow: I did not have a program to replace the structures that I challenged.

Now the program that I am learning urges me to accept. It urges me to love. It urges me to respect. All in all, it challenges me to grow up.

52.   13TH STEP

The 13th Step is taken by members who suffer from the delusion that sex can cure their addiction. Thirteenth Steppers are not always easy to spot. Some go to meetings and appear to work the Program, while others just sit around clubhouses, eyeballing members of the opposite sex (always newcomers), waiting for their chance to pounce. Newcomers, being somewhat bewildered, sometimes confuse lust with love and fall victim to this dangerous game.

Many newcomers have run from the Program when they realize the "help" being offered was a mask for sexual favors. Many of these unsuspecting newcomers never come back. Sex has never cured anyone's obsessions or addictions.

I am responsible for not using my experience in the Program to take advantage of a fellow member, especially a newcomer. If I see anyone 13th Stepping, I will do what I can to tell the person how unlucky the 13th Step is.

53. HERE TO HEAR— SPONSORSHIP I

"The most useful words a sponsor can utter are 'uh-huh'."

This is the first of two sponsorship guidelines that one of my sponsors developed over the years and it's always been useful for me.

As a sponsor I am first of all an ear. I am here to hear. I am here to encourage my sponsee to speak, to open up, to get it out, to cleanse the gunk from his mind, to bring it into the open, to expose it to the light of conversation (as opposed to keeping it hidden in the squirrel holes of the mental dark, where we dig up and rebury subjects with the frenzy of worried rodents). All in all, I am here to help my sponsee let go of whatever it is that threatens his sobriety.

In that respect the place where the two of us meet is always an open place. His home, my home, the coffee shop, a park, a car, wherever. In this place we are doing for the sponsee's mind what lower animals do for each other's bodies: we are grooming him, plucking out the mental ticks and fleas that bug him, holding them up, exclaiming "gotcha!", flicking the bugs away.

Sure, some problems take more work. Some problems are long-standing. Some problems may never go away. But for the most part, the things that drive us really crazy, and most seriously threaten our sobriety, are the little things, the things we need to let go of right away: what the boss said, what the kids did, what the wife insinuated, what that other driver was trying to do.

These are the kinds of things that can breed resentments, send us back to our squirrel holes for more scratching around. If given into, these are the kinds of things that can make us use again.

So I try never to turn down a sponsee when he calls or suggests getting together. No matter how together he sounds, I know he needs to talk now. Because he's called now. And once we start talking, I try never to steer what he's saying. I try always to listen to what's coming out of him. And I try to listen long enough to hear him say what he is going to do.

Sure. Most of us know exactly what our course of action should be. We just don't want to do it. Then we talk it out, get some light on it, and doing what we didn't want to do suddenly doesn't seem so bad after all. In fact, doing it, whatever our right action is, seems to be a hell of a lot smarter, and a hell of a lot less hurtful, than grimly, stubbornly, righteously hanging on.

If the sponsor can put the sponsee in touch with his god within, the god who knows the proper course of action, then the sponsor is promoting true growth. He's not putting splints on his sponsee's problems; instead, he is encouraging the sponsee to develop his own interior healing and his own interior change.

54.   HERE TO SERVE—SPONSORSHIP II

"The most useless words a sponsor can utter are advice."

This is the second guideline my sponsor gave me and it reinforces his conviction that our program is one of humility. It's a program of learning from each other and working things out together and always being willing to change our minds.

When it comes to this program, the only thing I know for certain is DDAGTM (Don't Drink And Go To Meetings). The rest—essentially changing our character—takes time. The rest is a process, a development. Our lives can't be fixed by one word, and certainly not by one person. In other words— and it's sometimes been a shock to me, especially in my early days—the sponsor is not God.

The sponsor is a humble servant. When I serve as a sponsor, I have to remember that I know very little indeed. I am not a marriage counselor. I'm not trained in child development. I know nothing about job placement. The only reason I am dealing with a sponsee is because he wants to stay clean and sober, because he wants to keep working his program.

Thus, when a sponsee and I get together, we discuss aspects of his life that affect his program. In such discussions, I have two main areas of knowledge. I know about mistakes and I know about solutions. *My* mistakes and *my* solutions. I know the wrongheaded things I did while I was using and I know the ways that I've been trying to work the Twelve Steps.

That's it. That's what I can share with my
sponsee. My experience, strength, and hope as a
recovering addict. If he's having a problem with his
wife, I can tell him about a problem I had with my
wife. If he's having a problem with his boss, I can
tell him about a problem I had with my boss. But
I can't tell him anything about his problem with his
wife. Ditto about his problem with his boss. Those
problems are his, not mine.

If he's having a problem with acceptance I can
talk about that. If he's having a problem with fear,
I can talk about that. I can talk about the emotional
and spiritual rehabilitation of this recovering addict.

But I cannot tell a sponsee what to do. As in my
sponsor's first sponsorship guideline, I cannot
threaten or impede the development of a sponsee's
relationship with his god within. What I can do is
encourage that relationship to grow.

55.   THE BENEFITS OF SHARING

Sharing is the basis of our program. The
absolute fundamental. Back in May of 1935, Bill W.
felt he would drink again if he didn't do some
honest sharing with another alcoholic. His subse-

quent meeting with Dr. Bob—the fact that each man was able not to drink because he was opening up to someone who understood him—became the taproot of our program. This is how we work. By sharing.

Not performing. Not pontificating. Not telling. Not knowing. Sharing. Finding out through sharing. The other night at a meeting a young woman finished up her comment by exclaiming, "Gosh! I didn't think I was going to say that. I didn't want to say that." She grinned. "But I guess I needed to say that."

And we needed to hear it. We needed to know that she'd been having trouble with the Third Step because, it turned out as the discussion went on, the rest of us had also been having trouble with the Third Step. None of us had been in Hollywood getting an Academy Award for Superior Third-Step Performance. None of us had all of the answers. Some of us had some of the answers. Together our meeting became a testament to ways that the Third Step can work.

Not *the* way. Some ways. Which we discovered together. Because we were there to share.

56.   IMPROVING RELATIONSHIPS

Love doesn't just sit there, like a stone; it has to be made, like bread, remade all the time, made new.
—Ursula K. LeGuin

We all probably believe our recovery Program will give us new chances to form relationships. This may be frightening to us because our experience with intimate friendships has been pretty rocky. They have been a source of much pain and misery for many of us. We have only to look around to see that for most people relationships are not easy.

When we work our Steps, we discover how much shame, guilt, pity, and anger we had for ourselves and our partners. We had invested enormous amounts of time, energy, and personal resources in those relationships. The Program has revealed a need to completely overhaul our attitudes about intimate and personal relations.

The Program has helped me be a better partner in a relationship. Most of the time I never really needed better partners. I just needed to be a better person.

57.   THE STATUE STARTS TO MOVE

When I went to treatment I resembled a statue.

Over the years of my using I had put on myself layers of protective coverings: protective habits, protective attitudes, protective behaviors. These coverings served to get me through my using life because they shielded me from most things that would have interfered with my using, such things as a committed career or caring relationships.

Like a statue I became a hard surface, and what I then sought out were other hard surfaces: jobs that did not involve me, people who did not make demands on me. My main thrust in life was to use, always to use, again and again, and my second thrust in life was to keep myself free of any en-tanglement that would threaten my using. These two forces of rigidity—to drink, and not to bother with anything else—made me resemble a rock-hard statue of which the only vibrant member was an arm, reaching out to fill the glass again.

Now that I'm in recovery, I spend a lot of time chipping away at this statue, attempting to dig out from the granite image I turned into something of the spontaneous youth who got trapped inside.

Now and again I run into this kid. He laughs before he frowns, accepts before he judges, says yes

instead of no. When things don't go his way, he
rebounds. (He's willing to change.) When he
doesn't know how to do something, he asks for
help. (He's willing to learn.) When he's afraid of
the future, he trusts in God. (He's willing to grow.)

After a few years in recovery I'm beginning to
gain a new image of myself, a positive image, and
it still resembles a rock, only now there's a sturdy
sapling splitting the stone apart.

Will this sapling mature into a tree? Only if I
keep chipping away at the remaining stone, only if
I keep freeing myself of the old self-protective,
self-defeating attitudes and behaviors that blocked
my growth. Only if I am willing to bend with the
forces of life will I grow, and blossom, and get my
roots out of the rock and back in living soil.

58. ACCEPTING CHANGE

For most of us addicts any sort of change is
difficult, often threatening.

We want the world to be as we expect it to be.
Solid. Steady. We want to get up in the morning
with our day in place. Predictable. Reassuring. If
there is a question anywhere in our day, say an
appointment that may or may not come off, we will
nag at that question either till we get it settled or,

most likely, till it unsettles us. All day long we will move through an otherwise smooth-flowing day with a dark cloud over our head because...

◆ We do not know.
◆ We cannot exert control.
◆ Once again, as always, we are not God.

Because we are not God, we have to work with other people. We have to accommodate other people into our schedules. We have to develop the ability not to make a big deal out of things, specifically the unpredictable things that other people do.

For the good of my soul and the good of my relationships and the general good of the day, I try to welcome change. Sometimes I even cultivate change. I ask my boss what he wants me to do. I ask those close to me what they want to do. And then—it's just like jumping in the ocean—I do it.

59. HOW TO ACT LIKE YOU'RE STILL USING

1. Never miss a chance to take yourself seriously.

2. Cherish your resentments.

3. Treat your partner as a sex object.

4. Treat your children and your friends as extensions of your ego.

5. Reserve deep affection for your pet or your car or your hobby or someone who lives far away.

6. Isolate rather than engage, quit rather than negotiate.

7. Fantasize about the ultimate humiliation of everyone against whom you cherish a resentment.

8. Don't do today what you can blame someone else for not having done tomorrow.

9. Employ behind-the-scenes manipulation whenever possible.

10. Feel sorry for yourself at least three times a day.

11. Be sure to point out other peoples' faults and failures. For their own good, of course.

12. Accept no authority but your own.

60. CHANGING ATTITUDES

The Program is education without graduation.
—Anonymous

We can never escape from reality. We must adapt to the real world no matter how different and difficult it seems. We can't change the *facts* of life, but we can change our *attitudes* toward them. That's the purpose of the Program, where we learn to cope without returning to the false courage and comfort of our addiction.

Stress and pressure are enemies of serenity. When they threaten to overcome us, we remember that they have been trying to make mankind escape into chemicals for ages. The healthy attitude we work for doesn't believe that stress and pressure come our way because "life isn't fair." It's important to our recovery that we remember, "We don't have attitudes; they have us."

I'm learning new attitudes toward old problems, and new solutions for them, by working my Program. I am learning to live in the real world.

61. CULTIVATING JOY

In a couple of weeks I'm going to do something fine. I'm going to New York City and I'm going to walk across the Brooklyn Bridge.

I'm going to walk over from Manhattan and have a cup of coffee in Brooklyn and then I'm going to turn around and walk back. I'm going to stand on that bridge in the middle of the air and watch the clouds sail over the city in the north and the ships sail by the Statue of Liberty in the south. I'm going to love everything I see because I'm going to be fully involved in life.

The first time I walked across the bridge—the pathway is a wide one in the middle of the span, one level above the roadway—a guy on a bicycle came up behind me, then zoomed down into Brooklyn. He was wearing a yellow baseball cap and he had a big green parrot on his shoulder.

Why not? Why not grab your bike and your bird and go for a ride in the air? Why not celebrate the fact that we are here? Why not have some fun?

After all the time and all the money and all the misery I spent trying to convince myself that using was the best way to go, it is grand just to be. Just to look around and take part and be happy enjoying the world as it is.

62.   OVERCOMING FEAR

"[P]eople get stuck in unwillingness, not inability."
— Dwight Lee Wolter

This is what unwillingness feels like to me: I have my arms that can do it, and I have my brain that can direct my arms to do it, but something has come down on my brain and my arms, something like a huge wobbly glob of plastic foam that encapsulates my brain and my arms and makes them mushy and useless. In such a state I start experiencing the old tunnel vision that could only ever see one solution, which was use.

But I don't use anymore, so now, when I feel unwilling, I do my using substitute. I drop out. I isolate. I indulge in some heavy-duty compulsive behavior, marathon TVing or sleeping or sex. Not to do the one thing I should do, I overdo something I don't need to do to prove...to prove what?

- ◆ that they can't push me around anymore.
- ◆ that I'm my own boss.
- ◆ that I'm the master of my destiny.
- ◆ that I am Chief Executive, King of the World, Supreme Being in a universe of one.

or

- ◆ that there is something wrong with the task.
- ◆ that there is something wrong with the person proposing the task.
- ◆ that there is something really wrong with any system that could allow such a stupid task or such a foolish person to exist.

or

- ◆ I just do it, and put an end to yet another bout of self-centered fear.

That's what my unwillingness stems from. Fear. Fear that what I do won't turn out my way. Fear that it won't turn out perfect. Fear that I won't get praised for doing it. Fear that I might have to stay late to do it or put off something else to do it or in some other way violate some plans I have made to do it. Fear that I won't be able to predict the outcome of doing it. Fear of the unknown, fear of the uncontrolled, fear of any scenario that is not worked out beforehand to guarantee me a certainty that I have only ever known one way before. By using.

Isn't this what always attracted us to our addictive behavior? That we knew what the result of our using would be? That we could count on the effect of our using with absolute certainty? That we could say, "Let there be euphoria and escape," and there was euphoria and escape? At the cost of everything else that we held dear.

Now we are back in the world, back to dealing with the everyday, the nitty-gritty, the stuff that needs to be done and needs to be accounted for and needs to be loved and cared for and held on to. The stuff that we are learning is dearer to us than our old euphorias ever were, stuff like waking up clean and sober and maintaining good relationships and getting some joy out of life as it is.

So I try to do it. I try just to do it. I try to stay in this world for the now.

63. NEEDING GOD

What did I think of God while I was drinking? Not much. Oh, I believed in God, but in the way that I believed in going barefoot to keep my soles calloused in the event of revolution. Believing in God was just another aspect of Being Prepared. Like the revolution, I never really thought that God would actually come, not in this life, and certainly not to me.

But it was not I who saved me from my drinking. All I did was go on a three-day binge, my first ever, and when I came to on a Sunday morning in my easy chair I had two thoughts. I thought that I could call a buddy to take me to the hospital. I thought that I could wait till noon when the liquor stores opened.

I called my buddy, and the rest became AA...

...through whose program I have learned that God did for me what I could not do for myself. God got this poor fool help for his drinking. God pulled me out of myself and the same old problems in which I'd sat, and stewed, and guzzled, for so many years. Through the program God reintroduced me to the good things of life: love and trust and care. The care of the Fellowship. The care of God.

Under this care I have been able to survive, even prosper, for nine years of sobriety, years in which I have learned not to fear so much, years in which the rebellious urgings of my ego have begun to be stilled by the voice of reason and the sound of sense.

Need God?

Yes. I need God, for whose presence in my life I daily thank the program and all my fellow travelers along this promised road.

64.   REBELS NO MORE

I've heard that some people never grow up—they just grow old. As a group, most of us were rebellious and defiant. We lived for excitement, kicks, and highs. We liked living "on the edge." We were outlaws from society. The fast lane wasn't fast enough. We weren't satisfied with getting high or too high; we wanted to be *way* too high. "Live fast, die young," was our motto.

For many of us, "acting out" got us in trouble with authority. We didn't like authority figures, or anyone who tried to influence our behavior. In recovery, we have learned that our rebellious attitude and behavior was just a sign of immaturity.

We became aware that our defiance and grandiosity had no place in recovery. Now we cooperate with life. We aren't banging our heads against walls anymore.

We've come to see rebellion as having no place in recovery. We don't want to be outlaws anymore.

65. RECOGNIZING CHANGE IN OURSELVES

Back in the days that I was God, I got up in the morning knowing What Must Be Done. Either I saw to it that My Momentous Tasks were accomplished, usually by someone else, or, if they were not accomplished, I found the person to blame. And that was *always* someone else. Then, as soon as I had time, I pulled the plug on the jug and sat down to congratulate myself for a job well done or belittle the jerk for a job botched up.

What this pattern of behavior came down to was a life of staying put. Being for the most part sodden, I could not grow. My roots were liquor-logged. Being locked into myself, I could not learn. I thought I knew everything already. And as for change, that was something which the other folks had better start doing to accommodate my holiness.

I mean, me? Actually change? In and of myself? Actually take the time and the patience and the care and, often, the audacity to seize a little nugget of discovering or hoping or wondering or feeling and turn that nugget into a new pattern of behavior? A new attitude? Something like a welcomeness to life?

Hey, that sounds like the program—and blessedly it is. Blessedly I have started, through the program, to realize the benefits of, and take part in, the process of change.

In this process I know first of all that life can be better than it ever was when I was using. The program has shown me that hands down. Next, my participation in meetings shows me that other folks are making remarkable changes in their lives, doing things like getting married or having children or buying homes or switching jobs or starting businesses or going back to school—big life-shaping changes which these people are able to accomplish not because they are acting above it all, like some goof's idea of God, but because they are being humble and grateful, like all the other real people they are going to for help.

Real people like me, who has changed to the point that he cares what happens in other people's lives. Most of the time. Sometimes I'm unwilling to care. Sometimes I want to stay put in myself. But then I think, that was what I used to do, and look what staying put did for me then. Nada. So now I try to come out of myself and ask what I can do for others.

I also care what's happening in my own life. I'm not throwing it away any more. I'm taking stock of what I'm able to do and admitting what I'm unable to do and in this process of getting down to right size I am finding out that life can be more exciting and challenging and just plain fun than it ever was when I knew every day at nine in the morning what I was going to be doing at six in the evening. Listening to the gurgle of despair that I was dumb enough to call joy.

Now, at six in the evening, I am sometimes with a friend, sometimes at a meeting, sometimes working in the garden, sometimes just sitting still and thanking God for the magnificent gift of being easy enough with myself and with others to seize and enjoy the moments as they come, and go, and shimmer with the vibrancy of time.

66. CREATURE COMFORTS

This is what I think at the zoo, in the penguin house. These birds have the pleasures of swimming and being fed and besides that they have the comfort of the company of creatures of their kind. Then I go to see the monkeys who are playing and sleeping and holding each other: the monkeys enjoy the comfort of the company of creatures of their kind. In the zoo cafe I tell the young man sweeping up that I like his red cap. "Thank you," he says. Then he turns to show me his employment badge. "If you don't have a job," he says, "you don't have nothing." Oh yes, I think to myself, it is good to have a job. It is good to work with others. It is good to have the comfort of the company of creatures of our kind.

Before I came into the program I knew I was an alcoholic but I did not think that condition qualified me for love. I thought that condition condemned me to the shame and horror that I felt toward myself every time I came out of it again. Each morning that I spent trying to paste my life back together I never thought that hanging out with a bunch of recovering alcoholics just like me would make me happier than I had ever been before. I never thought that my fellows could help me because, until I came to the program, I never let anybody in.

Now my arms and my heart can open wide because I have the sense to know that I too need the comfort of the company of creatures of my kind.

67. SHOULDN'T IT BE EASIER
THAN THIS?

It's been hard for me to accept that recovery is about progress, not perfection. I've been in the Program almost two years now and am still having my share of bad days. Hey, shouldn't it be easier than this?

I came into the Program thinking if I stopped using, things would be 100% better. I still think that way sometimes—all or nothing, black or white, yes or no.

When I get this way, I try to remember to quit looking for the magic. That makes my life much simpler. My doubts whether recovery is worth it are fewer. I realize that sobriety was just the first step; changing my life and how I deal with others and myself is the new hard part.

The times that are really bad are when I'm by myself too much, get into self-pity, and again think all or nothing. They say "an addict alone is in bad company." When I get like this I think, "What's the use?" I back myself into a corner of self-obsession and think there's no way out. I think I can't stand life's problems any more.

Then, suddenly, the Program provides an answer and the bad times pass. In this way, I'm learning how to live with my (new) self.

Before I came into the Program I really had no freedom. I didn't understand the word. The only things that gave me freedom were illusions—alcohol and drugs. So what I really was, when I thought I was being free, was a prisoner. The prisoner of active addiction who didn't know it.

I did know I was miserable, but I didn't know why. I thought I was under a curse. I was in a trap and desperate to get out. That meant I was at the mercy of other people's whims, and only knew how to be what I thought other people wanted me to be. I was always being blown around by the winds of circumstance.

The very first experience with freedom ever in my life was when someone said to me, "Do you want to stop drinking and drugging?" and I said, "Yes," realizing that I really meant it. The second experience was when someone said to me, "You need never get wasted again." Both these ideas had never before reached my brain and it was the first glimpse of reality and sanity for a really sick and desperate person.

The longer I stay in recovery, the more I learn about freedom. "Shouldn't it be easier than this?" is about freedom. Learning what's wrong with me is freedom. Becoming willing is about freedom. Changing is about freedom. All in all, it's not easy, but it's worth it, every Step of the way.

68. PRAISING GOD

When I first came in, I occasionally worried that the program didn't offer any formal ways of praising God. We didn't sing any hymns, we didn't recite any liturgy, the only prayers we said were the Our Father and the Serenity Prayer.

I don't remember how long it took, but one day I realized that the whole program offers me a way of praising God. Working the program *is* praising God, and I have the opportunity to do that however many hours of the day I'm awake.

I've often heard in meetings that GOD equals Good Orderly Direction, and so that's one of the ways that I praise God. I get up in the morning and do what I have to do. If something better or more interesting or more needful comes along, I do that instead. But the main point is, I'm prepared to be involved with the day. I'm prepared to go where the day takes me, so long as the path I follow is a responsible one.

I'm willing to listen to others, and try to understand their point of view. I don't throw a tantrum when someone can't do what I want them to do. I try to figure out how both our courses can be accommodated and still yield the best results for each of us. I try to participate instead of ruling the roost.

I'm not going through life like a steamroller any more, flattening everything out to conform to my way. Now I try to go through life like a seeder, spreading the good news of the input I get.

I work at the matter of living instead of trying to scam my way through. If I can't finish a job, I explain why I haven't finished instead of pretending that I have. Or pretending that the instructions were unclear. Or blaming someone else.

This is the way God means us to live, honestly cooperating with each other for the common good. I never understood that when I was using—and I certainly didn't act it. When I was using, I thought I was in competition with everybody else, from the other drivers in the morning to the other drunks at night. A friend who majored in anthropology once said that humans haven't gotten where we are by *competition*, the survival-of-the-fittest route. We've gotten where we are by *cooperation*, by helping each other learn new ways to do things, better ways to get through life.

God doesn't speak to us from burning bushes any more; he speaks to us from our fellows. So every time I go to a meeting or get together with my sponsor or friends, I am listening to people with individual faces and names and lives, and I am also listening to a force for **Good Orderly Direction**. Same for my meditative quiet times. Whenever I make the effort seriously to let the world fall away, I have the privilege of listening to God In Us.

Surely, all these ways of taking part in life are reasons for continual praise.

69.   THE LORD'S PRAYER AND THE 12 STEPS

A friend of mine who just came into the program asked me recently how AA could claim to be a spiritual rather than a religious program when every meeting was closed with the Lord's Prayer— straight from the King James version of the Bible, and part of many Christian religious services.

Here are my ideas of how the AA Steps are related to the Lord's Prayer.

We begin, "Our Father, Who art in heaven." Step Two is related to this, in that we "Came to believe that (there is) a Power greater than ourselves..."

"Thy will be done on earth..." Step Three is related to this, in which we become willing to "turn our will ... over to the care of God *as we understood Him*."

"Give us this day our daily bread." Again, this is Step Three, where we are willing to turn our lives over to the care of God. A little more explanation: The prayer does not say "Show us how to earn our daily bread"; it says that we are, in fact, putting our trust in God that He will provide for us—turning our lives over to His care.

"Forgive us our trespasses, as we forgive those who trespass against us." This is a biggie! The way in which we carry this out is in Steps Four through Ten. In these Steps we identify our own trespasses as well as what we perceive as trespasses against us, and we do something about all of them. In this process we relive our own conscience (forgive us our trespasses), and we unload our past resentments (as we forgive those who trespass against us).

"Lead us not into temptation, but deliver us from evil." It may not be stretching a point too fine to relate this to part of Steps Eleven and Twelve: "praying only for knowledge of His will for us and

the power to carry that out," and "tried ... to practice
these principles in all our affairs."

Finally, again we have a reaffirmation of our
faith in a power greater than ourselves, Step Two,
in "For Thine is the kingdom, and the power, and
the glory forever."

70.   THE VIRTUES OF ANONYMITY

One of the things I really like about meetings is
the amount of me I leave behind when I enter. I
leave behind what I drive and where I live, two big
factors of our identity in the outside world. I
haven't come to the meeting in order to work, so I
leave behind my resume. You don't pass around
photos of the wife and kids at meetings, so I leave
the family behind, too. When I enter a meeting I am
pretty much who I say I am when it comes time for
me to comment. I'm First Name Only, alcoholic
and drug abuser. I'm a man still locked in conflict
with the character defects that made him drink and
drug. I'm a human being in need of help from his
fellows and from God.

It's a real relief to concentrate on the stuff that
truly matters, the stuff that truly drives me nuts. Oh
sure, I may say in a meeting that the boss is on my

case, that the wife and kids are making unreasonable demands, but those people haven't come to the meeting. I can tell the group the really annoying thing that a guy in the hardware store did that afternoon, but the guy hasn't come to the meeting. I may even get into some old stuff about Mom and Dad and the grievous effect they had on their innocent little son. But Mom and Dad haven't come to the meeting.

I'm at the meeting. *I'm* the one who needs help. It's my character defects that allow me to get bent out of shape by what other people do. It's me who would rather whine than build character and so here I am where the whining stops and the character gets built. At a meeting. Alone. Naked of subterfuge and guile and self-defense. A quester on the road of spiritual achievement, and for that quest I don't need any of the trappings that I wear, and often hide inside, when I am out in the big world.

In my anonymity I am in my most defenseless, most helpable state. I am the essence of me, not any of the superficials. And because I pare down my existence to essentials in meetings, I can see clearly—maybe not for the whole hour, maybe not for half an hour or a quarter-hour, maybe not for even five minutes. But there will come a moment of clarity during a meeting when I am spiritually released from the worries that bind me, when I see how I should react or what I should do. When I rest easy in the knowledge of being loved by those about me who, like me, have gathered together to be helped by God.

Who also calls us by our first name. Because he knows who we truly are.

71. THE PROGRAM IN A NUTSHELL

I heard this at a meeting the other night: "The first three Steps are a gift. The last three Steps are maintenance. The Steps in between turn us into people who won't use again."

I can't quibble with that. Steps 1 and 2 came to me the instant that I asked for help: (1) I admitted I couldn't handle my life any more, and (2) God took over through treatment and AA.

Step 3 is a gift because it represents the bestowal of grace, but it was nonetheless a gift I had to work for. I had to break down and renounce a lot of old attitudes before the willingness to do God's will came to me. Oftentimes Step 3 remains a gift I have to work for because there's no guarantee that I will wake up willing every day. In this respect, I often work Steps 3 and 11 simultaneously, praying for both the willingness to work God's will and the power to do so.

Steps 4 through 9 are the Action Steps, and each one hurt, though not in any way that I could not stand. Each Step helped me get rid of some of the old me. Steps 4 and 5 represent getting right with self; Steps 6 and 7 represent getting right with God; and Steps 8 and 9 represent getting right with others.

In each of these action Steps I am working to define, understand, excise, and make amends for behavior which stemmed from the uncontrolled exercise of character defects. By writing out and admitting what I have done wrong I am asking for help and forgiveness from myself. By becoming willing to have God remove my character defects and asking Him to do so, I am asking God for help and forgiveness. By listing and making amends to the people I have harmed, I am asking them for help and forgiveness.

Remember that passage from the Twelve and Twelve, that we've never been able to form a true partnership with another human being? Here in the Action Steps we are forming new partnerships— with self, with God, with others. We are saying we are willing to work together, not skate by on illusions and unrealistic dreams.

We are saying we are willing to try again, and Steps 10 through 12 help us make our efforts stick by encouraging good relations with self in Step 10, good relations with God in Step 11, and good relations with others in Step 12.

It works.

72.   SAYING "NO"

The art of being wise is the art of knowing what to overlook.

—William James

One of our common goals in recovery is balance, a feeling of being centered. If we lean too far in one direction, we lose our balance and fall over. We can't please everyone. We can't be everything to everybody.   There is a balance the Program teaches us between selfishness and selflessness.

We need to be careful to organize our time and set priorities.   We can't sponsor everyone, be at every meeting, or volunteer for every service opportunity. Recovery is not a race to see who can do the most.   Easy Does It.   We need to learn and practice what are called "refusal skills." We need to learn when to say no. We have the right to refuse requests, to slow down and take time out, to take care of ourselves.

We let ourselves get too stressed out when we're not careful in scheduling our time.

73.   EASY DOES IT

I used to think I had to do everything myself. When I didn't do everything myself, or didn't do everything perfectly, I beat myself up for those failures. Sure I was a perfectionist. An obsessionist. An isolator. The kind of person who could be absolutely berserk inside his head while doing something so innocent as weeding the garden. Why? Because the garden had to be weeded by 2 p.m. so I could go to the greenhouse and fight off the hordes of ravening gardeners zooming in on exactly the perennials I wanted to buy and snatch them up right from under the noses of the ravening gardeners and....

Well, recovery has helped me get tired of this approach to life. Recovery has helped me understand that I don't have to do it all myself. That I don't have to project it all myself. That I don't have to live in a world that is bounded by the four walls of my mind.

The program says, Come out into the real world and see how well others take care of you. See how well God takes care of you. See that the world is not composed of the angels and fiends that you imagine. See that most people have always been doing what you are learning to do: get along with reasonable attainments and okay resolutions.

But what about ME?, cries my ego. What about winning the Saturday Afternoon Driving West Award for getting to the greenhouse by 2:10? What about winning the Western Greenhouse Award for finding and collecting and stacking on a table and paying for each and every perennial I want, all within the record time of eight minutes?

What about sitting down and having a soda and thanking God for helping send my ego south for the afternoon?

I'll take the latter course. I'll put my feet up. I'll say, "God, only you could create the world in seven days. It's taking me longer than seven days to do one garden. But after all, I'm not you any more."

Thank God.

74.   HELPING GOD HELP US

This is what I read in one of my recent morning meditations: God can't help us remove our character defects if we keep practicing them.

Like most of the rest of the program this statement is very simple. Why didn't I think of that before?, I say to myself, and the answer is: I didn't want to. In the words of Step 6, the first of the two defect-removal Steps, I wasn't ready to think that. I wasn't willing to take yet another flyer into the unknown, that free-floating world of happenings uncluttered by the squirrel-cages of my control. I wasn't willing to trust. I wasn't willing to learn or change. I wasn't even willing to be willing, and that is the first condition of working with God on any problem.

Oh sure, the naysayers say, being willing: that's just another way to say let God have His way. Let God win again. Let God tromp all over you. Turn you into the hole in the doughnut.

Well, hey: I'm certainly glad God did the doughnut-hole trick on my drinking. Since coming into AA I have not had a serious urge for a drink. That desire was lifted from me. Same for the desire to use drugs, but that took more time. That was harder. I had to work at that one. I had to show God I wanted to be drug-free, and I had to ask God for help on a daily, consistent basis, and most of all I had to mean what I said. I had to be willing to be released from that compulsion. I had to be convinced that drug use was not to my benefit. I had to say, I can't, You can, Please help me.

These days I'm working on the defects of gluttony and lust. These twin slobs follow me about day after day, blubbering for more. "You've given up drinking and you've given up drugging and you've given up smoking," they whine. "So why not indulge us? Why not take your ease with us?"

The reasons why I don't are all the same. Any excessive indulgence opens me up to feeling I can do it all, have it all, control it all, ego-whip the world with my will. And that kind of behavior doesn't work any more. I have to face the fact that I am not an ordinary guy (how I loved that distinction when I was drinking; how it drives me nuts now). I don't have built into my system the rational controls and stops and guards that other people have. I just want to go, go big, zoom off the launching pad like a missile when, most days, what is called for is a leisurely biplane trip along the Mississippi. A trip that incorporates the world instead of blowing it off.

The foxhole prayers never worked for my drinking and they won't work for any of my other character defects. I can't ask God to help me overcome my desire for potato chips when I'm finishing off another bag. I can't ask God to help me overcome my lust when I'm giving in to it again. I can't ask for help if I'm not willing to be helped.

I've got to do my part in order for God to do His.

75. BROKEN HEARTS

Many of us, during the course of our lives, experience a number of broken relationships. Some of them are very painful and stay with us for years. We often feel we have been harmed and hold onto deep resentments about the rejection. After many days, months, sometimes years, we bury our broken heart and carry on with our lives.

Step Eight asks us to take another look at these relationships. We must dig up our broken heart and assume our responsibility for our part in the break. We come to discover that, whether we like it or not, we all have a part in the breakdown of a relationship. The way to help us heal a broken relationship is to make amends. As hard as it may be for us, we must make every effort except where we may harm someone. We must be honest, even if it means the amends are not returned.

Today I try to remember that relationships always have two sides. I take responsibility for my part in broken ones, and make amends where I can to the best of my ability.

76. AVOIDING RELAPSES

If any men came to us with our records, we would want to help them. To guys dragging years of drinking and drugging and other obsessive behavior behind them, guys dragging a record of prison terms and failed relationships and kids somewhere or other, guys dragging job histories that never get off the ground, credit applications that keep getting denied, hope that keeps turning into despair, enjoyment that keeps turning into grief, days that keep turning into aimless, self-defeating nights: wouldn't we say to men like this, Please, let us help you?

Sure we would. And we *do* help such fellows, because we're in Twelve-Step programs now. We can see now that behavior like this does not work, that lives like these are grim treadmills that we ourselves wouldn't want to board again. We see this again and again, on the streets, in meetings, in our readings, in the investigations that we make of our own lives.

So why does the thought keep coming to us, Maybe it will work this time? Why, in the middle of a day when we have maybe gone to a meeting the night before and are planning on going to another meeting in a couple of hours, why does the thought suddenly cross our minds, Hey, a cold beer would taste good now. Hey, a line of coke would feel good now. Hey, I could handle a chocolate cake now. Hey, I could go to the track now, bet one race, and come right home again.

Why do such thoughts strike us? Probably because we're feeling good. Probably because something has gone right. Probably because that one good mood, or that one successful accomplishment is going straight to our heads, swelling our heads with conceit and cockiness, making us think again, I Am God, I Can Do It, I Can Do It All!

I can do so much, we think, that I can even survive doing the one thing that has brought me down every single time in the past.

Well, guess what? We *cannot* do the one thing that has brought us down every single time in the past. We know that now. We know ourselves now. We know we cannot have the cold beer. We know we cannot have the line of coke. We know we cannot have the chocolate cake. We know we cannot go to the races. Because we know, know absolutely, that that one thing will bring us down again. Without fail, it will bring us down. Every time, it will bring us down. And we have too much going for us now, even if it's just three days of sobriety, ever to threaten our good record again.

We want to get better, we want to stay better, we want, at last, after all our miseries and failures, to enjoy our lives.

Knowing ourselves this well, we practice the program. When the notion of using crosses our minds we immediately ask for help. Please God, we say, please help me overlook this dumb idea. If the thought persists—and usually it doesn't; usually it is just a passing fancy. But if the thought of using does persist, we *keep* asking for help. We ask our sponsor for help. We ask our buddies for help. We go to a meeting and ask those folks for help. We do some reading and get help that way. We get down on our knees and pray.

Whatever help we get, we are recognizing the one crucial fact of our new life in recovery. We are no longer in charge of our lives. We are not God. We cannot do it all.

It's a blooming miracle. We know ourselves now. We know we cannot do it all.

77.   THE POWER OF ACCEPTANCE

Many of my earlier memories are of trying very hard, with a small child's limited resources, to change the people, places, and things in my little life that were unacceptable to me. In fact, it seems that all my life I have pitted my strength and ingenuity against unacceptable situations, trying to change them into situations I could accept. The less they budged, the more frustrated I felt.

Even after I discovered alcohol's ability to erase situations unacceptable to me when sober— or to change my mood to fit into them—I was still faced with the hassle of having to sober up to struggle through unacceptable situations at home and at work. I became addicted to alcohol and to its illusion of power. It was the only agent of change I had. I also developed the stomach problems, backaches, tension headaches, and generally tense attitudes that define your basic Type A tilter at windmills.

I finally ran to the end of my own endurance and asked for help. My answer was Alcoholics Anonymous. I became free from alcohol but was faced once again with my old enemy, powerlessness over my life. I repeatedly heard and read in AA that we have to ask God for the serenity to accept the things we cannot change. I did, and would like to share the growth in acceptance that God has given me.

First I learned that I do not have to like something to accept it. I had assumed that in order to accept something, I had to condone it, agree with it, or otherwise change my attitude to conform with the position of the person, place, or thing. I found this unnecessary. It would not be growth for me to change to conform with some of the attitudes I encounter. It is growth, however, when I try to understand other people by listening to them, whether I agree with them or not. It is also growth when I admit to myself that I cannot change something or someone, and ask God for the courage to turn my thinking toward something I can change.

I have also learned that I do not have to choose something to accept it. I had come to believe that in order to accept something, I had to continue to allow it to be a part of my life. I've learned this is not true, either. I can accept certain people, places, or things exactly as they are, but still choose not to affiliate myself with them. I believe God does guide our choices when we turn our lives, and our wills over to him. I also believe that the power to choose is the only power I have.

I look at life now as if it were a cafeteria. I do not assume, when I get in line at a cafeteria, that everything offered there is for me. I am expected to make my choices from the selection offered. Do I criticize the roast beef simply because I'm in the mood for fish that day, or because my cholesterol is high and my physician recommends I avoid red meat? Perhaps the pie is unfitting for me because of obesity or diabetes, but do I have the right to say that pie is wrong for my friend who needs to add twenty pounds to her weight for her health's sake? By the same token, the career, life-style, or mate that may not be right for me may be perfect for the person sitting to my left at my next meeting.

Looking at things this way has freed me from having to justify to myself and to others my reasons for making certain choices. It forces me to be honest with myself about priorities. Most of all, it comforts me with the knowledge that God cares for me and my life and that, one day at a time, He is restoring me to sanity by granting me the serenity to accept those things I cannot change (but need to choose).

78.   HAVING ROOM FOR THE PAIN

Back when I was using, I would do anything not to feel pain. I would drink. Drug. Have sex. Sleep. Watch TV. Eat. Listen to music. Smoke. Go for an overnight trip. Go drink, drug, have sex, sleep, watch TV, eat, listen to music, smoke somewhere else. Then I'd turn around and come back home and do it all over again.

This pattern worked. I rarely felt pain. What else I rarely felt was joy. I never felt happy. I never felt serene. I was so obsessed with not feeling pain that I never felt calm. I was hyper from tranking myself out. I was like a Zombie who keeps getting jolted by electric shocks to prove that he's alive. And another name for Zombie is Walking Dead.

Take out the booze and the drugs, but add a whole mess of cigarettes, junk food, and coffee, and you've got the way I tranked myself out during my first years on the program. And that's okay, I see now, because, as we say, God never gives us more than we can handle. If, when I was new to the program, I had felt the pain I have recently come to feel, I would have been a serious candidate for relapse. I couldn't have handled the pain when I was first starting out. Like a toddler, I had to depend on my program friends for support, and on my baby fat of using substitutes for cushions when I walked, and stumbled, alone.

I had no room for much pain in my first program years, but now I am willing to let it in a little at a time. I am willing to admit now that I do not have what I would like to have. I am willing to admit that I've been wrong.

That's how change begins. With the willingness to accept the seed of need. Nowadays I need company, I need solace, I need cheer. (I cannot make myself feel good any more.) I need instruction, I need experience, I need knowledge. (I cannot make myself look smart any more.) I need recognition, I need approval, I need strokes. (I cannot reward myself any more.)

I need the Fellowship to help me lead a reasonable life.

I thank the Fellowship for being there for me. I thank the Fellowship for showing me how. I thank the Fellowship for helping me have room for the pain, and for providing me with solace and support when I start to feel overwhelmed.

79.   POWERLESS

Fourteen years before I came into the program, I admitted to myself I was an alcoholic. What I did not admit then—what I could not admit because the concept was alien to me—was that I was powerless over alcohol.

Me? Powerless? Oh no. I thought exactly the opposite. I thought that recognizing my alcoholism was empowering me to control it. Naming the monster was helping me put it on a leash.

Then I spent the next fourteen years being dragged down into hell by the monster who had *me* on a leash. The monster from whom only God and the program could finally set me free.

By the end, when I hit bottom, I was absolutely powerless to do anything but cry for help. I could not fix my life, or lie about my life, or pretend about my life any more. My life was a shambles and the only way that it could start to get better was for me to gain release from the monster that was ripping me up, and shredding me into pieces, and treading me into dust.

I could not drop the leash, not on my own, because denial made me think the leash was leading me somewhere. Denial made me think I needed the monster. Even as the monster was destroying me,

I thought the monster was my only friend. I was so sick I thought my suffering was love. I thought my destruction was life. I thought I needed to feel bad in order to feel good, and all I ever felt was worse.

Through the infinite, amazing grace of God, I was finally able to get out of myself just enough to call for help. And that call, plus holding on, was all it took.

God was there, the Fellowship was there, understanding doctors and counselors were there, family and friends were there. No one ever tried to tell me to go back to drinking. No one ever tried to tell me to keep using. Everybody said, "Welcome home. We've been waiting for you."

And what was it that I came home to? I came home to love. To the positive forces that unite people. To the helping, caring, nurturing relationships that I had turned my back on by trying to run my world on my own.

After so many years of being dragged through life by a monster, I finally let go. I dropped the leash. I stood there and watched the monster run away into nothingness. Then I turned back to the open arms of the program and got taken in.

By finally admitting I was powerless, I gained the most power I have ever known in my life. Much

more power than any booze or drug ever provided.
Through the program I have gained the power of love,
and that is a tie that binds which I will not let go.

80.   BELIEVING

When we surrendered to our Higher Power, the
journey began. Many of us had trouble believing
that a God existed when we began our recovery
program, because for years we thought we were the
master of our own affairs. We paid attention to no
desires or wishes but our own.

When we realized how much help we needed,
we first looked to other members and our group for
support. By rejecting at first the idea of a Power
higher than ourselves, many of us did accept the
idea of a Power *other* than ourselves. As we have
made spiritual progress, most of us now have a clear
and ongoing belief in a Higher Power that we call God.

It is important to our recovery to rely on God,
as our own belief in a Higher Power is what can and
does save us from our addiction. Only two of the
Steps talk about addiction. The other ten talk about
spiritual growth.

In recovery, we have a firm foundation for
spiritual health and spiritual progress when we
continue to believe in our Higher Power.

81. CAME, CAME TO, CAME TO BELIEVE

Over the years that I have been in the program, I have learned that all the slogans work, and the first slogan that really made sense to me was this variation on the Second Step: Came, came to, came to believe (that a power greater than ourselves could restore us to sanity). Here's how the slogan worked for me.

Came: That's all I did in the first year. I came to meetings. I did not know what was what. My life had completely turned around. I wasn't in charge of my life any more. I had lost control, but in a good sense, like a man whose craft is put on automatic pilot. I felt sure that I was going somewhere, I felt sure that the mission was on target, but I just did not know what the destination was. I had embarked on the biggest adventure I had ever known—living on God's time—but I had not learned how to tell that time yet, so I just sat still and looked out the windows and held my fellow travelers' hands and said the prayers they taught me.

Came to: Gradually, over the first year, and the second year, and the third year, I learned about the program. I learned to take care of the new vessel I was in. I learned the maintenance program of going to meetings, and I started to practice the Twelve major Steps that kept my working parts in order. I began to understand the ways I had left my old life behind, and I began to appreciate the fact that I could now do things I used to be afraid of trying. I was coming out of the fog of active substance abuse and into the clarity of self-knowledge.

Came to believe: After I made several happy landings—visiting people I'd been wary of, trying ventures I'd previously had no confidence for—I began to realize that the new vessel I was in was my very own life and I was able to maneuver that vessel in ways I'd only dreamed about before. I was learning not to fear, not to mistrust, not to prejudge, not in any way to prepare myself for doom. I was learning to let go, to surrender, to accept, to be—to live in the now without recourse to stewing over the past or fretting about the future.

I was learning to be fully human, and fully trusting, and that was nothing I had ever been able to do for myself. That was nothing I had even wanted to do for myself. I'd been too crazy. And now I could see that God and the Fellowship—my two higher powers—were indeed restoring me to the sanity my life had been lacking for so long.

How did I know I was getting sane? Because I was learning to accept higher powers in my life. Other higher powers. I was finally willing to admit I was not my own god.

82.   THE THIRD STEP

Back when I was a teenager I heard the folksinger Odetta at a nightclub. One of the songs she did was "He's Got the Whole World in His Hands." With the rest of the audience I clapped and swayed and hummed along, thinking how good and fine it was to hear about God's love.

Then I went away and got drunk for a number of years. Then I hit bottom and went into treatment and one day in art therapy the teacher asked us to represent the change in our attitudes since we started treatment. With crayons I drew a huge pair of wings whose feathers were scarlet and orange and gold. The teacher asked what my drawing signified. I replied that in recovery we are all riding on the wings of an angel.

I'm amazed that I could have had that insight after only two weeks in the program. Sometimes these days I have a hard time acknowledging the very same fact: that my life is in God's care. That, as Odetta sang, He has got me in His hands.

Some days I act like a frightened beast at the edge of the woods. I can't go back where I came from because something terrible is going on in there, something like a devastating fire. I have to keep coming forward. I have to keep trusting that the Power in this wider, open world is a loving Power, one that will accept me as I am, one that will help me grow.

Some days I still have failures of trust. Some days I still run away. You can see me toss my head and turn my tail and gallop back to the woods of self. I can stomp around in those woods for quite some time, bellowing Gimme!, bellowing Mine!, bellowing My Way!, bellowing Me! Me! Me! People in the meadows outside the woods wonder what is going on in there, what awful pain that poor beast is suffering. But it's only me, *El Stupido*, trying to play God again.

Trying, and failing, because even as I assert myself, have my ego fits and tantrums of self-will, I can smell the fires of destruction coming closer. Then I realize that the fire isn't in the woods. The fire was never in the woods. The fire has always been in me.

So out I come again, frolicking in the sunlight like a colt, happy to be taken care of in the meadows of love. My time in the woods has frightened me, so I hold on tighter than before, do more trusting, more sharing, more give and take.

Maybe I even allow myself to be tamed, accept a bit and bridle, start to give rides to others, start to help *them* through the world.

Maybe I even thank God for His care, for His patience and understanding, for His never forsaking me, for His always being there.

83. ALL OR NOTHING

All my life, everything was a question of "all or nothing"—job, school, relationships, possessions, obsessions, living, loving, and above all, drinking and drugging. No half-measures: totally wasted or white-knuckled abstinence. No half-pleasures: overworking or burnout. No half-treasures: money and security or broke and homeless.

If I couldn't win, I lost by giving up. Fight or flight. Victory or defeat. No surrender. No middle road. Just sad, bad, mad extremes.

So here is another paradox of the Program: As with my former life, so my new life in recovery must also be all or nothing. But this time it is positive, absolute abstinence from my addiction one day at a time—or death for all days. Today, the giving of my attitudes and will to my Higher Power and the principles of the Program must be all-out and complete.

If I am half-hearted about this, I may not be using today, but I'll be stuck and going nowhere. If I put all my energy into recovery, then—and here's the rub—everything else in my life today takes on the non-excessive, non-obsessive and non-depressive blessing of balance that some call serenity.

84. THE ASTOUNDING DISCOVERY

Some days I feel like Christopher Columbus, a voyager who has discovered a whole new world.

This new world has always been here; it was only closed to me. Only because I would not ask for help. I only had to say, "I can't handle it any more," and I was landed on another shore.

"How did you do it?" people asked when I was first in the program. "How did you give up drinking?"

I didn't give up drinking. I didn't do anything. It was God who lifted the merciless obsession from me. When I hit my bottom, and acknowledged that I had—when I said, "Help me, I have had enough"— I was set on a new ship, and steered to a new country, and allowed to disembark in a land that was strangely like the land I'd left. And yet completely different. All the joy I'd thought I was getting from a bottle shone instead in the eyes of the people who greeted me, and took me in, and showed me how to live as they lived, without suffering the onslaughts of fear and the tyranny of resentment and the misery of trying to live by my terms alone.

Why didn't I do this sooner? I wondered when I first came in. Then I learned the program better and realized that I had needed every drink, and every snort, and every other excess to reach the point of honest, helpless, total surrender. I was God's and he was mine and we were fine together. Through the love of the Fellowship, God was working on a whole new life for me, and for once in my career of self-direction, I was willing to let others show me the way. I was willing to enjoy the benefits of commerce, both spiritual and social. I was willing to be part of the journey.

Hey. Columbus didn't get himself a raft and a compass and a goatskin of water and go paddle off to the new world alone. I did not come to my new world alone. All I said was, Let's go, and three brave frigates of endeavor, Steps One and Two and Three—my *Niña* and *Pinta* and *Santa Maria*—

showed me how to get here, and stay here, and say thank you every morning for the trip.

85.   I OWE IT TO STEPS 1, 2, 3

I would be nowhere without the first three Steps. I would be dead, or a wet-brain, or the babbling drunk at the end of the bar. I could well be homeless, evicted by my drinking to sleep on the streets. I could be hopeless, someone for whom the telephone does not work. (I call, the line is busy; I call, they can't talk; I call, they do not answer.) I could be without God because I am too far gone in misery to accept God. I could be utterly, absolutely, despairingly alone.

But I am none of these things because I have the first three Steps.

The First Step brought me everything I needed. It brought me the first word of that Step. It brought me We. It brought a concept of life completely overwhelming to this egomaniac; it brought a life that depends on the input of others. If I don't understand how to do something today, I don't get drunk to show the problem who's boss. If I don't get my way at work today, I don't get drunk at home to get my way tonight. If I am lonely, I don't get drunk to prove I don't need anyone.

I go to a meeting and talk it out.

I call my sponsor and talk it out.

I accept the fact I'm human, and imperfect, and talk it out.

The Second Step brought me the God of my understanding. During all my drinking years I had forgotten about God. Never in my life had I understood God. I had heard in church that God is Love but I had thought those words were just some kind of spiritual commercial, some feel-good hype.

Then God got me out of the drinking. God saved my life and saved my butt and I was standing there saved and—well, I'm alcoholic. My first words were not Thank you. My first word was Why? Why me, God? I asked. Why save me?

The only answer that has ever come to me is love.

Certainly there is nothing God can get out of *me* but love. I can't buy God dinner, or a drink, or get Him a date. All I can do is thank Him for the rest of my days. All I can do is love Him for the rest of my days. And the gratitude and love I feel for God tells me in return that He loves me. I have made a connection with a Power greater than myself and I never want to let that go.

Which is why I do Step Three. To keep God in my life. To keep the primary fool (me) *out* of my life. To keep moving in a path that makes me feel better than my old paths. The paths that led me into the dark and over the hill and down to the swamps of despair.

Now when I get up in the morning, I try as best I can to turn my will and my life over to the care of God. Then I stay out of the way. That's the main point to turning it over—*keeping* it turned over.

When I start threatening my own recovery or my own serenity by asking for things it is not in my power to give me—things like justice or recognition—then I call for help. I go right back to the First Step, admit my life is unmanageable, and inquire of others how to straighten it out. I pray to God for the ability to leave it alone till it straightens itself out.

Above all I trust.

And get busy with something else.

And smile.

86.   STILL GROWING

A lot of the things that bother me these days are things that bothered me when I was eight.

I'm not kidding. It embarrasses me, but it's true.

I always wanted my friends to do things my way. Play my games. If they didn't, I sometimes went along with them. But not usually. Usually, when I didn't get my way, I went home. Sulked. Watched TV. Read. Felt sorry for myself. Teased my sister. Bullied my brother. Nagged Mom.

Sounds like a real dry drunk, doesn't it? The eight-year-old egomaniac stomping around the house wreaking havoc because he has the sulks. Egging everybody on till he gets smacked, and sent to his room where he spends fifteen minutes screaming and bawling and kicking the wall, then half an hour plotting his revenge: leaving home, or burning down the house, or getting discovered by a talent scout for Disney. Then he sleeps it off. Then he wakens terrified that he will lose everyone he has been plotting to lose. Then he figures out how to restore himself to everyone's good graces—and he does, because he is a cunning little kid.

Last Saturday I had to go in to work. When I got there, resentful at having to give up weekend time, I misunderstood a note left by a coworker. I thought the work I'd come in to do had been done. It was eight o'clock Saturday morning and I was at work for—for nothing!

I was so angry I threw a book across the room. I stomped down the hall past the bulletin board. Then I turned around and ripped papers off the bulletin board. A chair was out of place so I sent that sailing, too. Then I went back to my desk to write Everyone A Memo, but I'd cut my thumb with a pushpin defoliating the bulletin board, and I was bleeding on my desk. It was a lovely summer morning, the sun was streaming in the windows, and I was standing in the middle of a tantrum mess, sucking my thumb.

I'm thirty-eight years old.

God grant me the ability to accept the things I cannot change, courage to change the things I can, and the wisdom to know the difference.

I bandaged my thumb. I picked up the papers, crawled around on the floor till I found all the sprung pushpins, restored the bulletin board. I unwedged the chair from between two desks and put the book back. I sat down at my desk and wiped up the blood.

Then I called a program friend and told him what I'd done. We laughed a long time.

When I hung up, the sun was still streaming in the windows. I pretty much knew what it took another phone call to find out—that I had misunderstood which work needed doing.

Me? Wrong?

After leaving work at noon I stopped by the bakery where I placed a Monday morning order for Everybody's Favorite Muffins.

Thank you, God, for the ability to learn. And remember. And connect. And laugh at myself.

87.   IS THIS THE WAY THAT GROWN MEN BEHAVE?

At my men's home group meeting last week, one of the guys gave a lead on fear. I'll call him Curt. One of Curt's clients has recently changed distribution methods and Curt had to call the firm to find out if they would still be needing his services.

As he told it, Curt was faced with making a call to hear No. To Get Rejected. To suffer the first major downhill step in what would surely turn out to be the ruination of his career.

Did Curt make the call?

Not on Friday, because everyone is looking forward to the weekend on Friday. Not on Monday, because everyone is recovering from the weekend on Monday. Tuesday would have been a good day to call, but Curt forgot about the call on Tuesday, and Wednesday, and by the time he remembered to make the call on Thursday it was almost Friday, when everyone would be looking forward to the weekend.

It took Curt two weeks to make his call, and when he did, finally, heart in his throat and palms sweaty, his contact said she'd been waiting to hear from him. She said she was hoping they could do business together. She wanted Curt to come in ASAP.

We all laughed along with Curt about his construction of disaster, and then we went around our circle of seven detailing incidents that dovetailed with Curt's. Each of us told how we had been frightened of the unknown, then more frightened of the bogeys we made up for ourselves, then paralyzed by our self-induced paranoia and anxiety.

Back when I was growing up, I thought men got together to compete with each other. (Sports.) I thought men got together to have fun with each other. (Drinking.) I thought men got together to work with each other. (Making money.)

I never thought that men got together to care about each other, to help each other out, to love each other back to health.

I'm glad the world has changed, and I'm glad I belong to these changes. I'm glad we end each home group meeting by holding hands and saying the Lord's Prayer. I'm glad we hug each other goodbye. I'm glad none of us is afraid of loving each other. I'm glad we have the courage, and the simplicity, and the dedication to be each other's friends.

88. LEARNING TO TRUST

I've been in recovery six months now, and I really don't understand that much about the Program. But I can say, I have more faith now than when I came in. I think one of the first things I said to my sponsor was, "I don't get it." I didn't understand what recovery was going to help me with, except not using. Who or what to believe? My old friends and ways of doing things? I was still full of myself and starved for any meaning in my life.

When I said to my sponsor, "I don't get it," he answered, "Why do you have to? If you don't understand why the sky is blue, does that make the sky a different color? Just because you don't understand what recovery is all about, does that make the Program less helpful?"

I was looking for proof and have found out that I need to just believe and to trust. Step Two asked me for faith, to accept that the Program works without instant proof, and to be able to ask my Higher Power for help with my problems. I began to use my Higher Power before I really understood it.

For instance, when I hear stories from those who decide to "go out" and try using again, I don't have to follow their example in order to prove them right or wrong. I can trust their experience. The only proof I need that the Program works is to look to my sponsor and all the other members, and listen to their stories of how it was and how it is now. Faith in the power of the Steps reminds me that one of them begins, "Came to believe...." Unless I stick to my belief and faith in the Steps, I am in danger of maybe relapsing or staying stuck, wondering why the sky is blue.

89.   MAKING AMENDS

Yesterday I had a letter from a friend, replying to an amend I made. He had not known that I was alcoholic. While that fact helped to explain the hurt I had done him, it was obvious that part of him is still hurt, and still does not understand my behavior.

Right now part of *me* is hurt. Part of me does not understand my behavior. Since I got my friend's letter, part of me has been looking out windows and staring at the floor. I haven't been feeling sorry, either for myself or for him, and I haven't been being angry, either. I haven't been constructing further amends or further justifications. What I have been doing is growing.

Through my friend's eyes, I have been back in direct contact with the person that I was when I was drinking. I have been feeling how it was for other people when I went powerhousing through their lives. Asserting the Mega Me. I've been reliving my experiences with my friend through his point of view. I've been thanking him for never telling me off.

It wasn't so much that I did terrible things, though there were a few episodes that wouldn't win an etiquette prize. What was worst, as I remember it, and feel it now, was a pretty consistent lack of concern for my friend. A totally self-centered, selfish point of view. I was like a record, displaying what looked like thousands of grooves, but no matter which one my friend put the needle on, the groove was always playing my song. The groove always led back to the center, which was me. And the center always held a hole, which was my inability to look beyond myself.

Right now I'm sorrier than I was when I first wrote to my friend, and that is as it should be. I know that my letter caused him to relive pain. Now his reply has caused me to understand and take part in pain, both the pain I caused him and did not understand at the time, and the pain I feel now over the opportunities for friendliness that I denied us both.

One of these days I'll get it right, and because of his letter I am learning how. This is how God speaks to us—through others—and I am very glad that my amend to my friend allowed me to hear what God has to say. I understand now, deeply and sincerely, that if I don't have the courage to face the negative things I have done in the past, I cannot look forward to fulfillment of the promises in the future.

"Painstaking." That's the way the Big Book puts it. "If we are painstaking about this phase of our development [making amends], we will be amazed before we are halfway through. We are going to know a new freedom and a new happiness."

All I can say today is that I am getting ready for that happy freedom. And as far as this recovering person is concerned, that's a big step in the right direction.

90.   IF IT AIN'T BROKE, DON'T FIX IT

I've just been out in the garden, lifting up squash leaves and looking for zucchini. It's the first week of August and I have had only one zucchini all summer. The plants produce lots of flowers, and lots of little baby zucchinis, but they always turn yellow and wither before they mature.

I bought these seeds from a new place. I didn't need to, because the seeds from the old place worked fine. I had zucchini all summer long. But last winter I was seduced by some trendy marketing, the implication that if I planted seeds from this new company I would have a better reputation among people who are accustomed to dining in Europe.

Huh? I'm a hungry recovering drunk who wants some zucchini in America. I want it cut up in salads, and cut up in yoghurt. I want to cook it with onions and garlic. I want to stir-fry it with other veggies. But I don't have it. Because I decided to fix it. Because I decided to make my zucchini perfect.

This has been the story of my life—going one or more steps beyond what is necessary, or even desirable, in order to polish, augment, put my mark on something that was okay just the way it was. Something that worked fine—until I came along to make it Extra Special. And in the process turned it away from its vital roots.

I've done this with friendship—not saying, Oh, what the hell, and going along with the gang.

I've done this with love—waiting and waiting and waiting for conditions to be absolutely right before I made my first move, by which time I'd lost the opportunity for doing anything but constructing a monument to my Intention to Move.

The problem here is essentially one of playing God. Making predetermined plans and conceiving predetermined notions and living my life in dreams of perfection instead of in reality.

What I've got out there in the garden now is like one of the fantasies I make up for myself. The zucchini plants look great. They look healthy and happy and bursting with fruit. But when you lift up the leaves all you see is wizzly little yellow stumps drooping in the dirt.

My plans for perfection can lead to great appearances. But without the vital input of others they do not yield reality. All they yield is disappointment. A hollow shell devoid of content.

Oh Lord, help me to let the life in. Help me to let life work just the way it is. Help me not to fix things. Help me just to let them be.

91.   RENOUNCING THE RAT RACE

I once watched a program about Al Jolson, in which a man who had known the famous singer was explaining what a big ego he had. If Jolson was about to give a performance, and he heard that a new dry cleaner's was opening down the street, Jolson would be jealous. He would be offended that the cleaner's was opening on the very same day that he was doing a show. He would become convinced that the cleaner's was out to get him, to ruin his career.

We have a lot of terms for this malady in the program. Terminal uniqueness. King Baby. The egomaniac with the inferiority complex. A universe of one.

I know all those terms very well. I can suffer from one or the other at least once a day.

I sit in my office stewing that I have not heard from a friend. I examine the reasons he has not called. I decide he doesn't want to talk to me any more. I get angry with my friend. I vow never to call him again.

I hear that someone else in the company has gotten a promotion. Well, there goes my career. I go through the reasons why that person's promotion will mean my dismissal. I call my wife. I tell her to update my resume.

The neighbors buy a new hose. That hose really irks me. It's a lot better than our hose. And their old one didn't look that bad. What do they need a new hose for anyway? Why are they always sprucing things up? A-hah! Because they're going to put their house on the market. They're going to sell to a family with quadruplet teenage punk rockers.

There goes the neighborhood.

There goes my serenity.

There goes my ego again, bound to the boulder of my competitiveness, rolling me down the hill again, sploosh! into the swamp of despair.

I don't have to be on top to be happy. I don't have to be in the news to be real. I don't have to pause every hour of my life to take a curtain call.

I don't have to regard the people who are trying to live or work with me as potential threats. In fact, it would be a whole lot better for my life and my career if I regarded them as actual friends. If I *treated* them as friends. Instead of skulking about the forests of my mind, aiming arrows of vengeance at them with my addled will.

My addled self-centered will. My addled self-centered competitive will.

Come on, guy, I say to myself. What are you doing in recovery anyway? Then I answer myself: I'm working the Steps of a program whose first word is We.

So I call my friend and find out that he and his wife have been in Hawaii for two weeks. When I get home I get their postcard.

I call the person who got promoted and extend my congratulations. We arrange to have lunch to discuss ways our departments can work together better.

I say to my neighbor, Hey, you guys got a new hose. Yeah, he says. Our daughter sliced up the old one with the mower.

The world is a welcome place when I treat it as such. It's a hostile competitive rat-race when I treat it as such.

It's my life. It's my choice. It's my well-being.

Today I will try to treat the world with love. And I will try to remember that that world includes me.

92.   GLAMORIZING

I'm slipping when I begin to remember more of the good times than the bad. We must keep our memories of the years Before the Program in proper perspective. By the grace of God the compulsion was released from us. However, the addiction was not; it is always waiting for us to lower our guard. A danger sign we watch for is the voice that rewrites our past history.

The scenes we remember are parties, new partners, romance, laughter, music, sex, ballgames, intimate conversations, poolside play, Sunday brunch, getting ready to go out and "party hearty." Seldom do we remember the bleary-eyed mornings, the waking up with strangers, the embarrassments, the lost jobs, wrecked cars, wet beds, the toilet-hugging, the divorce that broke our hearts.

When my addiction talks to me about the good times, I need to remember "the rest of the story."

93.   HOW ABOUT OKAY?

The more I drank the more I disliked myself. The more I disliked myself the more I drank. In order to justify this self-defeating, self-hating behavior, I told myself that most people weren't any different. If they didn't drink, they drugged, and if they didn't drug, they overate, and if they didn't overeat, they fooled around, and if they didn't fool around, they were probably dead. Right?

Wrong.

There are lots of people in this world who are comfortable with themselves. Who have learned to take care of themselves and the other people in their lives. Who have learned to live on reasonable terms. Sure, these people have their faults. There are things in their lives they'd like to change. They'd like to have more money, or more time, or more hair. But they don't beat themselves up about these things. They don't compensate themselves to the point of stupor, or terror, or death, because they haven't got these things. They don't say to themselves, you are just as bad as a devil, but because I have the abilities of a god, I will make you feel as powerful as me—until you come to in the morning, when you will feel just as rotten as you have every right to expect, you nasty devil, you.

Up and down, and up and down, and up and down, the trials of duality go on. Good/bad, right/wrong, high/low, in/out, here/there, yes/no.

Hey! How about okay?

Instead of feeling like Zeus on Mount Olympus, or the lowliest scum of the earth, how about feeling like a regular guy? A doer and a schlepper and a taker of care. A guy who gets things done, and relaxes, and has a good time, and goes to bed, and gets up to get some more things done, after which he relaxes and has some more fun. He does this without subjecting his behavior to the scrutiny of the Inquisition. He doesn't contact Ann Landers or Dr. Ruth or the Supreme Court to get a judgment on his every act or thought. He gets to the point of knowing what makes him feel useful and happy and worthwhile and he tries to stay with the behavior that produces those effects.

Sometimes such a guy is a guy on the program. Depends how well he's working his program. Depends if he is willing to settle for okay.

94. LOVING LIFE

I know I didn't love life when I was using. In those days I treated life as an enemy. One on whom I had to practice tricks, or manipulation, or evasion. Convinced from the instant I woke up that life was not going to go my way, I plotted out my stealthy approach. I made careful plans for getting what I

wanted from life—booze or drugs or sex or money—
and equally careful plans for scurrying back with
my booty to my cave.

In my using days, I was always operating from
an *on* perspective: *on* the lookout, *on* the lie, *on* the
make, *on* the defensive. I was rarely living from an
in perspective: *in* the swim, *in* the know, *in* the now,
in the thick of things.

I was always holding back, waiting for my way
to come true. I was never jumping in, finding out
that my way could be the way that life was carrying
me along.

I am very sorry these days for all the opportunities I missed, opportunities for love and joy, for
learning and trying and testing myself, for providing myself with a background of achievement and
knowledge to rely on and consult.

But I am also glad I feel sorry. On good days
I welcome my remorse. Because my remorse
shows me what I must not do now.

Sure, there are still times when I behave like a
suspicious caveman, peering out at life from the
deep cover of self-bondage. I'm too dumb to
realize I feel this way when I wake up, and by the
time I can name the form of self-bondage I'm
suffering from today—fear, self-pity, anger—my

naming doesn't matter because this time I *know* I'm right. I know everything the suspicious caveman in me is whispering: that my enemies are lurking in the woods behind me, in the plains before me, in the earth below me, in the sky above. Right?

Wrong.

In most cases, probably all, what I dub enemies are really spirits of love, and they are *challenging* me to come out of myself and say I am here. They are *challenging* me to take part. To savor the now. To make the now as good as I can. To love life as it happens.

To say Wow! To say thank you. Thank You, God, for this challenge. Help me, God, to accept this challenge. Help me to love life every blessed day.

95.   LEARNING FROM OTHERS

When I lived alone with my bottle and my bull I thought I knew everything. In truth, I was living alone with my bottle and my bull so I could know nothing. I was living alone with my bottle and my bull so no one else would ever question my authority. For over twelve years of using I kept the soap bubble of my invincibility afloat. Then one morning reality stuck a pin in the bubble. Splat!, like that, I hit my bottom, and my godhood was over.

So I came into recovery and began to learn the many ways that I had functioned as my own worst enemy. I also began to learn the many ways I can *still* function as my own worst enemy. That's because I've been going to meetings and hearing other people talk about the same character defects I suffer from.

At the beginning I thought these people were very strange, confessing stuff I wouldn't even have admitted to myself. In the words of the Twelve and Twelve, "Who wishes to be rigorously honest...? Who wants to confess his faults to another and make restitution for harm done?"

Not me. I wanted to climb back into my active addiction and make the world go away. Even more, I wanted to make *me* go away. And guess what? That's just what the program has done. Gradually I have learned that the program *can* make me go away. First, it gives me something to think about other than myself. Secondly, it helps me accept and work through my negative self-defeating thoughts and behavior. And for the most part it helps me achieve these two goals by presenting me with examples of how other people are making positive, patient improvement in their lives.

I sit in meetings and listen to me. Sometimes I'm a middle-aged woman, sometimes I'm a teenager. There I am, noodling around in my mind, and suddenly, someone else is describing my life. A problem with ego. A problem with letting go. A problem with accepting change.

I listen in. I listen to what the other people say the problem is, and I listen to the ways they describe for solving the problem. I keep listening as the comments go around because other people are picking up on this problem, saying how they've suffered from it and what they have done.

When the meeting is over, I rarely go right home and apply just what I have heard to my problem. Life is more gradual than that. But I begin to be willing to let go of some of my jerkiness because, having learned that it doesn't work for other people, I am also understanding that it does not work for me. Having heard other people open up, I'm also willing to do some opening up myself. Maybe I call my sponsor. Maybe I call a buddy. Maybe I talk to my girlfriend.

But I'm not alone anymore. I'm not God anymore. It used to be that the jerk in me was always threatening to jump out and ride around on my back shouting "I'm the boss!" But through the program and through God and through my own good efforts, I am learning to keep the jerk in his place. I am learning that being rigorously honest is a lot better way of life than being an arrogant know-it-all who has no one to talk to but himself.

I may not open like a flower every morning, but I sure don't close down like a dumpster every night.

96. MEETINGS

It takes the good and bad meeting—the good and bad speaker—to make the Program work. We are told that every meeting we attend will be a good meeting. Our sponsors will tell us that there are no bad meetings; all meetings are good, some are just better than others. Newcomers are asked not to even consider whether the meetings are good or bad. "Just bring your body and the mind will follow," and "take what you need and leave the rest."

Even when we think we didn't get much out of a meeting, we will find that many others who were there benefited a great deal. We may remember something we heard at a "bad" meeting more often than what we heard at a "good" meeting. The old-timers tell us, "The most important part of any meeting, for you, is the moment you walk through the door into it. It's not so much what you do there, it's the fact that you are there."

Today I remember that some meetings may be better than others, but it's more important that I'm there.

97.   MY SPONSOR

When I was in the Program only a short time, it was suggested I find a sponsor, a person who had the kind of recovery I wanted. The reason for finding a sponsor was to have someone who would guide me through the 12 Steps and help me apply the tools of the Program to problems I would come across.

I finally asked a guy at my home group. I was a little hesitant because he was 40 (pretty old), and what would we have in common? But I asked him, and he agreed to be my sponsor.

I soon found out that our age difference of 18 years didn't really matter. The first time we got together, he picked me up to go have coffee. He was listening to a Def Leopard tape, which really blew me away. We talked about one of the songs on the tape, *Foolin'*. When I was using and loaded, I used to take a song and think I was singing it, that I was one of the band members, and the words were my words. That song summed up my life before recovery. "Is anybody out there? Does anybody care?" I was so full of self-pity, that was my theme song. We had a long talk about living in rock 'n roll lyrics, especially that song. So that's how my relationship with my sponsor began, and it's lasted for over two years.

I've found in recovery that there *is* "somebody out there," and I've found a sponsor and fellow members who "really care." I'm not on the pity pot any more. Sponsorship is one of the important ways of carrying the message. Sponsors share freely their experience of working the Program. They don't nag or manage our lives. At times, sponsors may appear to be very strict, but they're only trying to pass on their knowledge.

Now I'm a sponsor, and helping my sponsee also helps me. Thinking about my sponsee reminds me: I need to return his Pink Floyd tapes. Or are they my sponsor's?

98.   NEEDING OTHERS

I had one friend before recovery. I had one entertainment. I had one joy.

To feel happy and at peace with the world, I needed to travel no more than five blocks. Then I was with my friend. Five blocks back, and I could bring my friend home. This was not a long way to go, so I made my trips often, by car and on foot, in all kinds of weather. The winter of 1979 I walked down the middle of the avenue in a blizzard because I needed my friend so much. I needed so much to feel good that I made myself sick going out for my friend, and once we were home alone together I made myself sick all over again.

I don't have that friend any more. I don't have that entertainment. I don't have that terrible frightening joy.

Now I have another kind of pain, and another kind of joy. It's called being human, and I still run from this condition more than I embrace it. I still seek to pretend it isn't there more than I accept it. I still maintain a posture of being above it all—while underneath it all I am crying for help.

I am crying for help because I am learning to live again. I am learning basic facts of social interaction, and to my great relief I have a learning school to go to. It's called the Fellowship.

This Fellowship is the most important part of my life. Here I have finally met the people who know how to treat me as I am. Not as I would like to be but as I am. These people understand that I'm the kind of guy who appears to wear his heart lightly, while all the time, inside, his heart is throbbing like a nuclear device. Some sort of James Bond gizmo that can blow up the world with emotion—fear and hate and all the shades of human turmoil in between—if....

- ◆ If I don't go to a meeting.
- ◆ If I don't unload.
- ◆ If I don't share.
- ◆ If I don't name my secrets.
- ◆ If I don't let go.

Most people are glad to spend blizzards inside. Most people don't walk down avenues in swirling snow squalls to buy something that will make them feel warm inside. During blizzards most people *are* warm inside. Because they are staying where they are. At home. Close to other folks who are there in the flesh or at the end of the phone.

Dear God, help me to stay where I am: in the grips of my humanity, where, as long as I respect them, and need them, and trust them, everybody's name is fellowship.

99.   GETTING BETTER, NOT PERFECT

Over the past couple of years, I have been learning to enjoy the company of others, sometimes to seek it out, and I've been able to do this because I have been relaxing my fantastic expectations.

I often think back on a weekend I spent with a sister and brother last spring. None of us wrote a concerto. None of us pitched a perfect game. None of us solved The Problems of Childhood. We didn't even discuss the problems of childhood. We got together in a city where none of us live and we went to museums and we went to restaurants and we went to the circus. Then we traveled back to our own homes in other states feeling lucky to have been together. Because we helped each other have fun.

"Is that all there is?" cries the stressed-out, Type A superachiever who lives in part of my being. "Having fun?"

"What more do you want?" replies the laid-back, Type B program person I am trying to become.

Type A: I want to produce the circus. I want to direct the circus. I want to star in the circus. I want to fling myself across the air on a trapeze and I want to catch myself when I let go.

Type B: That ain't possible, guy. You need someone else to catch you when you let go.

Type A: Well, what about if I practice real hard? What about if I set one trapeze in motion over there and then swing back over here and set this other trapeze in motion and then...?

Type B: And then stand there watching two trapezes swinging back and forth?

Type A: I'm sure there's a way to do it. If only I think hard enough.

Type B: I'm sure there's no way to do it. So give up thinking and ask for help.

Type A: What about if I punish myself? What about if I deny myself all sorts of things I need or would like to have till I solve my problem? Wouldn't that work? Then I could reward myself lavishly when I solve the problem. Or I could finally admit that being unable to solve the problem is someone else's fault—probably my parents'—and then I could lavishly solace myself for all the grief I have endured.

Type B: Why not just accept reality and not bother with the problem in the first place?

Type A: That would be too easy.

Type B: No one ever promised you a bed of nails.

Type A: Oh.

That's something I learned this spring. I can
make my life miserable, which I often do by isolating, or I can get together with some other people and
have some fun. And I can pretty much guarantee we
will have fun if I renounce unrealistic expectations
from them, or from myself, or from the things we do.

I can be normal. One of the guys. A regular
fella. A friendly dude.

If I just don't try so hard.

100.   THE QUANTUM LEAP

Yesterday I went to a new meeting and the
secretary was a fellow I haven't seen for six months
or so. His lead sounded good. He sounded like he
was pulling his life together. He was doing something that I hadn't heard from him before—using
program slogans and program phrases—and that,
to me, indicated he was learning from others. It
indicated he had become *willing* to learn from
others. That he was climbing up the ladder of
Fellowship success.

I've seen this happen often over my years in the
program: the quantum leap that people make when
they get it. When they start working it. When they
start becoming one of us. And the way they do it is

the way the program tells us to do it: they insert the key of willingness, and the door opens to a pathway that works.

This is the crucial point, the point at which the proud and the arrogant stick up their noses and turn away. I know, because I was one of those people for my first thirty-two years. I could stick up my nose and turn away faster than a speedball can whiz by a batter. I could be by you before you ever knew who I was, or where I'd come from, and all you would feel from my passage was the chill of the empty, arrogant air.

Then, one day, I needed help. One day I could not do it on my own. Again. The first time I needed help, the first time I could not do it on my own, was when I could not control my drinking. So I came to the program and found that help existed. That letting go of my insistence on my own way could bring positive results.

Then I pretty much forgot all of that, even while I kept coming to meetings. I started taking back control, and knowing everything, and taking other people's inventories, and blaming everybody else, from the pediatrician who delivered me to the director of the inpatient program that saved me.

I was miserable. Here I was, free of booze and free of drugs, and I was stomping around in my mind like a bratty tennis player protesting a call. The game wasn't going my way. I wasn't winning. Or so it seemed.

And it seemed that way because I was making judgments based on my past experience (you know: that wonderful time, when I had just about killed myself with booze and drugs and stupidity). I was not being willing to suspend judgments, as the program advised me to do. I was not being willing just to go along.

No. I was standing on some lofty perch, alone, knowing everything, rather than being down on the ground, among others, learning just a few things, one day at a time, things like humility, and gratitude, and trust.

Pain made me do it. Pain made me hold out my hands again. Pain made me say out loud "I need help." I said this to my sponsor and I said this to my home group and they smiled and nodded and told me how they'd been through the same pain themselves. And how they'd survived. By hanging on and turning it over and being willing to learn and change.

So I did it and it worked and I'm happy.

Not all the time. I can still make myself miserable by doing all the dumb things I did when I was first in the program. And I do, but not so often as before. I'm learning. I'm changing. I am, finally, completely, with absolute conviction, utterly unwilling to undo the quantum leap I made when I finally said I cannot do it on my own.

101. PROBLEMS HAPPEN

Today was rough, but that's O.K. I used to have years that were rough.

—Anonymous

Problems happen whether we are in recovery or not. Recovery does not guarantee us a life free from struggle, pain, or problems. It's not a direct flight to a magically safe place. When we got into our recovery program, the world did not stop and salute us. Recovery is about learning to exist in a world where crummy things can happen.

We are given tools that help us deal with life. The more we use the tools, the better we can live with life's realities and cope. The 12 Steps, good sponsorship, service work, and especially meetings are tools. Choosing a home group, having a sponsor, and attending meetings gives us an ever-present opportunity to handle problems and be with people who can help us. When we have problems and bad days, we no longer need to deal with them by ourselves.

Now, when problems come and upset us, we get help and talk about them.

102.   WHO'S IN CHARGE?

I made a big mistake a long time ago. I decided I was in charge.

I was still in college when I started acting on this decision, and the results were disastrous. I drank myself into a ten-year ego fit, with only dreams and schemes, not accomplishments, to bolster that ego; I burned bridges behind each step of my working life (every time I quit, I was going to "show them"); and I was five hundred bucks away from homelessness when I finally bottomed out. Bringing myself to the brink of despair—that was the best I could do when I was in charge.

How did I direct my life in those seeming days of power? The way most of us did, with the maximum indulgence and the minimum discipline. Thus I never cared, particularly, what job I had. I made no plans for a career. All I did was make up schemes to manipulate my job to my private ends. My *immediate* private ends. Could I come in late?

Could I leave early? Could I take long, lush lunches? Did I have plenty of other folks to blame? Could I keep myself covered while I did my own thing?

In my private life, I tried to regulate relationships according to the same maximum/minimum balance. How could I get what I wanted without giving up too much? How could I capitalize on my partner's vulnerability while protecting myself? How could I make sure that the control was in my name? How could I guarantee we would never have meatloaf, or parsnips, or tea?

This approach to life which I constructed was completely itsy-bitsy, square-by-square. I had no concept of the big picture (career, marriage, family, house—the whole ball of wax). I could only see the dots, the little bits of sticking-plaster joy I slapped on each day. My three solid drinks before dinner. My whatever it was that I ate. My beers until I went to bed. Or passed out on the couch. My Tuesday night with the current girl-friend. My Saturday night.

Our Saturday night? Sure. If she had a wedding to go to, with booze I didn't have to pay for. If she could score some cheap dope. If she would play according to my self-indulgent rules, there was nothing I wouldn't do for her. Except commit.

So here I am now, sober. I'm between relationships, and my job is just okay. But I'm happier than I've ever been before. Because I'm no longer calling the shots. Because I've surrendered control. Because I'm not trying to do it on my own. Because I'm letting go and letting God.

Because I am not in charge.

103.   STEP FOUR

We've got to face the mess we made of things some time or other, and it might as well be now. We're not going to get any better stewing in the mess and from what we hear at meetings we know we can get better—a whole lot better—by becoming willing to consider the ways we went wrong and the reasons why.

We know. We've always known. We just haven't wanted to admit it. We've tried to justify ourselves and explain away our actions and blame others for our actions till we were blue in the face— just like little kids holding their breaths till they get their own way. So everybody sits around and waits till the kid finally lets go, and starts to breathe again, and starts getting on with the maturing process of making his life mesh with other people's lives.

Same with us. We cannot hold it in any more. We have to let go. To breathe, to breathe freely, to keep breathing in the joy and the beauty and the common sense of life, we have to acknowledge that our way didn't work. We have to spell out the reasons why in a Fourth-Step inventory.

Why didn't our way work? Mostly because we put ourselves first. Because we wouldn't consider other people. Because we wouldn't incorporate their hopes and aspirations and realities into our tornado path through life. Ka-zooom! There we went. Leaving wreckage all around.

Now it's time to go back and look at the wreckage. Figure out the various overwhelming, self-centered urges and desires and instances of willfulness that helped to produce the wreckage. Start coming to grips with the fact that 1), we do have character defects and 2), those defects have been responsible for self-destruction in our lives. And unhappiness in a lot of other people's lives.

As far as I know, no one has ever been executed for his Fourth-Step inventory. No one has been led into a public square and made to mount a scaffold and there been hanged or beheaded or shot for having failed in the business of living with and loving others. The Fourth-Step process is not—

repeat, not—a punishment process. Rather, it's the beginning of a liberation process, the liberation from a lifetime of behavior that has alienated others and defeated us.

It's the beginning of freedom from pain.

104. AN AA MEMBER'S "CREDO"

I am glad to be part of Alcoholics Anonymous, of that great fellowship which is spreading all over the world. I am only one of many AAs, but I am one. I am grateful to be living at this time, when I can help AA to grow, when it needs me to put my shoulder to the wheel and help keep the message going.

I am glad to be able to be useful, to have a reason for living, to have a purpose in life. I want to lose my life in this wonderful fellowship and so find it again. I need the AA Principles for the development of the buried life within me, that good life which I had misplaced but which I found again in AA. This life within me is growing slowly but surely, with setbacks and mistakes, but still developing. I cannot yet know what it will be, but I know that it will be good. That's all I want to know, it will be good.

AA may be human in its organization, but it is divine in its purpose. The purpose is to point me toward the God of my understanding and the good life. My feet have been set upon the right path. I feel it in the depths of my being. I am going in the right direction with my fellow travelers. The future can be safely left to my Higher Power. Whatever the future holds, it cannot be too much for me to bear. I have the Divine Power with me, to carry me through everything that may happen.

Participating in the privileges of the AA fellowship, I shall share in the responsibilities, taking it upon myself to carry my fair share of the load, not grudgingly but joyfully. I am deeply grateful for the privileges I enjoy because of my membership in this great Way of Life. It puts a responsibility on me that I will not leave undone. I will gladly carry my fair share of the burdens. Because of the joy of doing them, they will no longer be burdens but opportunities.

I shall not wait to be drafted for service to my fellow AA members, but I shall volunteer. I shall accept every opportunity to work for AA as a challenge and I shall do my best to accept every challenge and perform my service as best as I can. I will be loyal in my attendance, generous in my giving, kind in my criticism, creative in my suggestions, loving in my attitude. I will give AA my interest, my enthusiasm, my devotion, and most of all myself to the best of my ability.

We in Alcoholics Anonymous know the joy of giving. We believe that when we come to the end of our lives, it will be only the things that we have given away that we will take with us. We will take no material thing with us, but we will take with us the kind words we have said, the kind deeds we have done, the help we have given. We alcoholics, who have been helped to find AA by someone who was interested in our welfare, believe that we are under a deep obligation to pass on the AA message to others. We members of Alcoholics Anonymous believe in this with all our hearts and minds: If an active or recovering alcoholic needs our help and asks for our help: "I am my brother's keeper."

105. IT ALL COMES DOWN TO US

Throughout my using life I wondered why I wasn't making it. Why wasn't I succeeding? Why wasn't I getting good jobs? Why wasn't I making money and driving a new car and owning my own home? Why wasn't I doing that? I kept wondering. Why wasn't I getting ahead?

Then I crashed and came into a program whose first word is we.

That's it, folks. That's the whole ball of wax. We. That's what I was missing all my drinking life. And pretty much all the ego-centered life that went before.

When it came to the inclusion of other people in my life, I didn't have a clue.

I don't mean dating and I don't mean being friendly and I don't mean being polite during Thanksgiving dinner or a job interview.

I mean being willing to let other people into my life. To incorporate them. To hold them dear. To need them and want them and cherish them. To get to know them and understand them. To hang around with them. To go to them as a spring creek rushes down a hill to a pool, where it finds solace and togetherness and peace. To feel one with other people and, through them, to feel one with God.

Twenty-five years ago an old lady said to me, "I always discuss my decisions with at least three other people. One family, two friends."

I thought that old girl was nuts. Straight out of her white-haired gourd. I was in my teens then, and I knew everything. I didn't need to ask anybody how to do anything. I knew what was right for me.

So the old lady died and I became a drunk and I did not have a clue why my life was a mess until the program showed me that no one knows everything. That everyone needs help. That everyone can benefit from talking things over with others. That the decisions which one makes alone are usually wrong. That I am not God.

That's what the old lady was trying to tell me. To lay off my ego for a guide and go to others who had more experience and knowledge and perspective. Trust what they had to say. On trust alone, do what they recommend.

I couldn't. I could not do that. I was too proud. Too stubborn. Too willful. And too cunning. So cunning that I could make any self-serving act look good. Sound good. Get perfectly reasonable people to nod their heads as I climbed out on another limb and sawed it off behind me. Correction. As I got good and tight, *then* climbed out on another limb and sawed it off behind me. As I came to on the ground, all smashed up again, and got good and tight as fast as I could to disguise the pain.

"Oh I'm fine!" I called to people who happened to notice I had fallen again. "But they sure don't make trees the way they used to."

The making of fools, however, follows the same old recipe:

a. Refuse to mature.
b. Become a smart aleck.
c. Reject all authority.
d. Substitute substance abuse for social interaction.
e. Make a jerk of yourself.
f. Whine when you get caught.

As far as human life goes, there is nothing else but people. Oh sure, there are plants and trees and animals and islands where one could live alone like Robinson Crusoe. But that's not the way it works, so we might as well stop pretending that we'd like life to be something else and accept it as it is. A people-filled proposition. A proposition which daily, hourly, sometimes minute by minute calls for us to interact with and depend on what other people say and do.

And if the proposition doesn't call for this interaction, we're probably using. Or employing a using substitute.

So I've learned some lessons. I've learned that people give me jobs. Dreams don't give me jobs. Neither do fantasies or wish-fulfillment scenarios. People give me jobs. Other people. People I have to interact with and get to know and maintain good relationships with. These people who give me jobs judge me on the skills I have, and one of the most important skills I have, as far as an employer is concerned, is getting along with others. Working with others. Is this guy a team player, employers want to know, or is he just a selfish s.o.b.?

If he's the former, we can probably advance him (thereby helping him get a good car and a decent home). If he's the latter, but has work skills, we can probably use him in a lower-level job (where he can keep making payments on the same old car and the same old home).

Unless we've got super brains or super talent or super money we're going to have to live in this world on terms which others have helped to make and which we have to cooperate with. These others are suffering from the same facts we are: that none of us possesses super brains or super talent or super money and thus we all have to work together for a living. Which in most cases means we have to get along with others. Which means we have to be decent folks. Which means we have to work our program as well as we can.

Which means don't use, go to meetings, and thereby change our lives around.

All the success or failure I've encountered in this life has depended on my ability to open up to and cooperate with other people. As my old friend pointed out, I have never made a bad mistake when I have talked things out or worked things out with others. I have made the most serious mistakes, the most harmful, uncorrectable, lasting mistakes, when I have acted on my own.

God, keep me from me. God, keep me with others. God, keep us working together.

106. PAST MISTAKES

If you turn it over and don't let go of it, you'll be upside down.

—Anonymous

A lot of unhappiness comes from dwelling on past mistakes and failures. Our Higher Power can do many things for us: remove a lifelong compulsion to drink, to drug, to overeat, to gamble; remove all kinds of character defects such as lying, cheating, stealing, adultery. God can determine many things, but our Higher Power cannot force us to accept our past. If we choose to walk around with shame and guilt about the past, that's our choice.

It has been the collective wisdom of our Fellowship that many people have relapsed because they couldn't let go and accept their past mistakes. We all, each one of us, were born imperfect. It is not surprising that this imperfection, along with our addiction, has caused us trouble along the way.

We learn how to live with past mistakes by practicing and using the tools of our Program.

107.   OUTLOOK OF TWO AA MEMBERS

Don D. went to an AA meeting one evening. He frowned when a member mispronounced a few words while reading "How It Works." He felt appalled when another member stood up and said he was an alcoholic and an addict. Another person talked too long. As he slipped out the door immediately after the meeting, he muttered, "That was terrible. I should have stayed home."

Bob M. went to a meeting one evening. His head was bowed as he listened to the "Preamble" and "How It Works." His eyes moistened as he listened intently to a member tell his story. He was grateful for being able to attend this meeting. After clean-up and a little socializing, he paused, and as he locked the meeting room door, his thoughts were, "Thank God for such a beautiful fellowship."

Both AA members were at the same meeting. Each found what they were looking for.

108. BEING POWERLESS

Before I started using, when I was still a kid, I sensed that I would not be a powerful person. I sensed that I would not have a powerful position in the world, or a powerful lot of money, or a powerful lot of happiness.

Until I came to the program, I did not understand that the powerlessness which I foresaw for myself when I was young would turn out to be *exactly* the measure of my adult happiness. When I was young, and when I was not young but drunk, I thought I *had* to have power to be happy. As usual, when I was young, and not young but drunk, I was wrong.

Today it's good to be humble. It's good to let go and let God. It's good to find out what the outcome is by living life, rather than crouch in a corner like a mad terrorist plotting devious moves to make *my* outcome come out.

The only place my outcomes ever come out is my head. Whereas, when I am truly living life, when I am truly in there being spontaneous and letting things go and living in the moment and not forcing my will or my ego on people, places, or things: hey, life is a trip.

And I'm no old hippie. I haven't traded in my love beads and pot for the pablum of propriety. I'm not getting "high on life." I live like most of us live, happy sometimes, sometimes grouchy, wanting more than I get, and complaining about more than I show gratitude for.

But every now and then, like boarding a little jet and taking off into the wild blue yonder, I am happy. I am happy to be free of the dreadful duty of being responsible for everything that happens. And everyone who does it. I am happy to be free of judging me, and judging you, and judging the United Nations. I am happy to be God's creature praising the joy of life.

And I don't have to be on vacation to feel this way. I don't have to be at home to feel this way. I don't have to be shoving all the beads on my abacus to the profit side. I can be doing something so simple as walking across the office when the sun comes up (I start work early). Some days that golden light hitting the southeast wall makes me want to sing. Once I turned a somersault. Usually I just stand at the window thanking God.

I thank God for the day, for my life, for the fact I have a job, for the fact I'm doing some good work, and having some good fun, and getting some joy out of life.

What else is there?

We know. But we don't need that any more. We don't need the pain of making ourselves feel good. We don't need the anguish of controlling situations or relationships or pointless, hopeless, ego-ridden schemes.

What we need now *is* now, the joy of the sun coming up—which is all the sun ever does, all over the world, all day long. All night, too.

If we allow the sensation to develop in us, and stay with us, we know that we are always in the tender care of God.

109. THE KEY'S IN YOUR OWN POCKET

The other day at a meeting, one of the tough guys began to talk. At first I rolled my eyes, expecting the usual macho, hard-core doctrine. To my surprise, something else happened. He began to gently talk about friends he had known over the years who had returned to drinking. Some had died as a result. He went on to say that each of us has different amounts of pain to deal with in life, and that he could not judge what was happening inside a man's soul. His voice was full of acceptance, serenity, a certain sadness, a gentle authority. At that moment, he had what I was looking for.

My frantic journey has taken me to many diverse places, into the heart of black suicidal despair, to bridges at night, and gun stores in the daylight. I have sat up nights, drunk, rocking in a chair in a lonely hotel room, chain-smoking and filled with fear. There was a time when I would run miles and miles every day, as if trying to reach heaven on foot.

For a year, I went door to door trying to spiritually enlighten others, hoping to force God into returning the favor, driven by a thousand forms of rage, an addict looking for that external substance, person, clue, anything, that would complete me. I was like a baby in a crib, the world revolving around me like a toy mobile above my head, or so I thought. I wailed and cried, but no one came, and in my egocentric anger I began to blame.

In the 1960s I began blaming in earnest. My first target was "the system," a popular choice in those days. Then my blaming was refined to my parents, teachers, God, and a long list of other targets. Blame is seductive. It enabled me to see the world outside and the people in it as bullies, and keep untarnished my self-image as the angelic innocent. Blame kept the focus away from the humbling, but vital, realization of my own mortality, limitations, and relative powerlessness. Jesus Christ said it best: "When you see that your companion has a splinter in his eye, first take the beam out of your own eye that you may see clearly to take the splinter out of his eye."

When I first read this passage, years ago, I understood it in a very different way than I do now. Then I thought He was saying that my faults and shortcomings were proportionately more numerous than my fellows, like a beam to a splinter. But now I realize the analogy is about directing one's personal energy where it will do the most good. In reality, my influence over others is very limited compared to the opportunity for change that lies within myself.

At first it may seem easier to avoid the inner journey altogether, to spend one's life running for election, being a slave to fashion, searching for the Holy Grail, for the golden key. But when all is said and done, the key was in your own pocket all along.

110.   A BREED APART

The longer I'm in the program, the more I feel that I belong to a breed apart. Certainly I still surprise myself, after many years on the program, by suddenly acting like the monster I used to be when I was using—a monster who, most times of most days, I mistakenly believe I have put behind me.

What this monster in me wants is his way. Right now. I think that I have disciplined the monster, made him nice and caring and concerned about others, and shazaam! Someone violates my private space in the checkout line and I turn around and glare. Someone cuts in front of me on the highway and I try to pass him at all costs. Someone at work contradicts a suggestion I have made and I'm ready to fire him.

My way still comes first. My first ego-ridden reaction to almost any situation is still: is this what I want? (Oh, sure, sometimes I have to sit there and try to figure out what I want. And sometimes—there has been this bit of growth—I get tired of trying to figure out what I want and just let events happen.)

But this easy-going attitude is still pretty rare. I do not take disagreement lightly. I do not take cooperation easily. I take myself far too seriously.

I often wear the world, not like a loose garment, but like a water-soaked blanket. I still make a big deal out of things which other people just brush off or ignore.

So I need the program every day. If the monster in me ever gets really loose, and really operative, I run the risk of using. I run the risk of taking back control, and grandiosity, and out-of-whack perspectives, and the my-way-at-any-cost kind of thinking that will let me drink and drug again.

Maybe the monster rises up for the same reason drinking dreams recur: to remind me I am never cured, just given a temporary reprieve. To make me know I need the program. To send me running back to a meeting asking for help.

111.   FORGIVENESS

When we join in an act of forgiveness, we bring relationships whole again. Forgiveness is not a state of mind. It is a state of being. If we do not forgive deep within our hearts, we have not really forgiven. Forgiveness which stays up in the head is really only the intention to forgive.

We know we have not truly forgiven when we can't forget what caused our resentments. If this wound is still open and sore, we did not forgive

from the heart. We remember to give ourselves
time, talk with our sponsor and fellow members,
and pray for help. It is good to share our resentment
in a meeting and ask for suggestions. Finally we
must wait. God will heal the wound in time *if
we let Him*.

Our willingness is the key. If we're willing to
let go, we will be given the power to truly forgive.

112.   WOMEN AS FRIENDS

I've been in recovery for 12 years now, or
should I say, I'm *back* 12 years. That's how they
say it in meetings in New York City. It means I tried
recovery once before, lasted three months, then
relapsed. That relapse was a nightmare, and has
motivated me many times to remember my last
drunk, especially in the first few years of coming
back to the program.

My first wife used "benevolent coercion" to get
me into an outpatient recovery program. I went
through the drill, went to meetings, but relapsed
after three months. All hell broke loose, and when
she gave me the ultimatum—sobriety or leave—I
just packed up and split.

In retrospect, I now realize I wasn't married to
my wife; I was married to *alcohol*. After three

drinks, something in my brain would announce that I wasn't married any more. I would become a self-centered, anger-driven, charming hustler. Massage parlors, strippers, and girlfriends. I had plenty of money and an endless supply of drugs to manipulate women into granting me sexual favors. And you know, they all said I was the greatest and that they loved me. In my fantasy chemical fog, I was able to be *truly* in love with not only my wife, but various other women at the same time!

So there I was, relapsed, separated, living in a small furnished apartment. But I was free to drink and chase women. In a binge, I flew to Reno and married again two days after my divorce came through. Things were going to be okay now, since *this* wife drank and used as much as I did.

They say when you go back out after a shot at recovery, things can get real bad and crazy. That was exactly what happened to me. As I said, that year of renewed drinking and a new wife was a nightmare. I ended up in long-term treatment. This was my second bottom and produced more financial loss.

The first year of recovery was very bumpy, even though Wife #2 was also in recovery. The biggest shock came when she relapsed. This was the most difficult situation I've faced in recovery. Was my recovery based on her recovery or my own? With the help of my sponsor and friends in recovery, I moved out and got a divorce a year later. There I was, in my late thirties, with two marriages in the toilet, and absolutely no idea how to relate to women.

Over a period of time, I learned I needed to treat women differently, not as objects for my power or sexual use. My self-image was so low, I couldn't imagine anyone going out with me just for myself and not for the money or drugs I could offer. Here's what I've learned:

1.   Dating can be fun and not frightening. I learned a new way of cooperative dating that doesn't include the self-centered expectation of the Three Ds: Dinner, Dance, and Drop Your Pants.

2.   Fear of sexual performance can be worked through. Responsible sex is good, and as the Big Book says at page 69: "We remembered always that our sex powers were God-given and therefore good, neither to be used lightly or selfishly nor to be despised and loathed." And I'm aware of the many relapse stories I've heard about guys using again when faced with a sexual opportunity, and drinking

because they were worried about performance without chemical help.

3. I've treated women with new respect. I've learned to become friends with them. And in one of the paradoxes of the program, by treating women with respect and friendliness, I'm making Ninth Step amends to those women I used during my active addiction.

I've spent many unpleasant moments marinating in the juices of past regrets over women I didn't treat right before recovery. Those periods are few and far between now, because whenever I get inside my own head looking backwards, I know I'm behind enemy lines. I don't Thirteenth Step women in the program. I did that a few times early on in recovery, and was straightened out by a sponsor who pointed out that I was supposed to share "experience, strength, and hope," *not* "experience, sex, and hope."

Now, at 12 years in the program, it looks like I'll be married again soon. By learning from my mistakes and following wise counsel, I think this one will work out. I've grown up, become a different man and better person because of slow, patient improvement in recovery and by learning how to become friends with women.

113.   SPIRITUAL RATHER THAN RELIGIOUS

A Simple Way Of Living

People who are recovering from alcoholism or other addictions through Twelve Step programs hear phrases such as "the spiritual part of the program" or "this is a spiritual program." Twelve Step programs clearly separate themselves from religions and, yet, are equally clear in claiming to be spiritual programs. What does it mean to be "spiritual rather than religious"?

One simple way of understanding spirituality is to see that it is concerned with our ability, through our attitudes and actions, to relate to others, to ourselves, and to God as we understand Him. All of us, addicted or not, have a way of relating to our own lives, other people, and God which tends either to be positive, healthy, fulfilling and life-giving, or tends toward the negative, self-defeating, and destructive. The question is not whether we will be spiritual, but whether we are moving in the direction of a negative or positive spirituality.

Spirituality is a simple way of living. It seems there are four basic movements that recovering people need to make to put their lives on a positive spiritual basis. The first of these is a movement from fear to trust; the second, from self-pity to gratitude; the third, from resentment to acceptance; and the fourth, from dishonesty to honesty.

114. DON'T GIVE UP

If there's one thing I want to pass on to those who are struggling in recovery, it's "don't give up." Like me, a lot of people come into the Program after spending most of their lives "giving up," running away from situations that were too painful or required too much effort. It was easier to quit and find fault with things we didn't like.

It's easy to give up on a problem too quickly. A long effort at finding a solution is sometimes painful and irritating. But we learn by working the 12 Steps that the answers do come if we continue to do the research—through study and prayer, one day at a time.

Courage is what makes us do the right thing even when we want to give up. We can find happiness while surrounded by darkness; we can be kind in the middle of hate and jealousy; we can have peace of mind when we're surrounded by confusion, fear, and anger. What has helped me is knowing and remembering that I *can* handle, with my Higher Power, fellow members, and myself, what I couldn't handle before.

I'm not a quitter or a loser any more.

115. SLOGANS

1. Easy Does It
2. First Things First
3. Live And Let Live
4. But For The Grace Of God
5. Think . . . Think . . . Think
6. One Day At A Time
7. Let Go And Let God
8. K.I.S.S.—Keep It Simple, Stupid
9. Act As If . . .
10. This Too Shall Pass
11. Expect A Miracle
12. I Can't . . . God Can . . . I Think I'll Let Him
13. If It Works . . . Don't Fix It
14. Keep Coming Back . . . It Works If You Work It, It Won't If You Don't
15. Stick With The Winners
16. Identify Don't Compare
17. Recovery Is A Journey, Not A Destination

18. H.O.W. = Honesty, Openmindedness, Willingness
19. Poor Me . . . Poor Me . . . Pour Me Another Drink
20. To Thine Own Self Be True
21. I Came; I Came To; I Came To Believe
22. Live In The NOW
23. If God Seems Far Away, Who Moved?
24. Turn It Over
25. Utilize, Don't Analyze
26. Nothing Is So Bad, Relapse Won't Make It Worse
27. We Are Only As Sick As Our Secrets
28. Drop The Rock
29. Be Part Of The Solution, Not The Problem
30. Sponsors: Have One—Use One—Be One
31. I Can't Handle It God; You Take Over
32. Keep An Open Mind
33. It Works—It Really Does!
34. Willingness Is The Key
35. Don't Quit—Surrender
36. Hugs, Not Drugs
37. Clean And Serene
38. No Pain . . . No Gain
39. Go For It
40. Principles Before Personalities

41. Do It Sober
42. Screw Guilt
43. Just For Today
44. Sober 'N Crazy
45. Pass It On
46. N.U.T.S. = Not Using The Steps
47. S.O.B.E.R. = Son Of A Bitch, Everything's Real
48. Before You Say: I Can't . . . Say: I'll Try
49. Don't Quit 5 Minutes Before The Miracle Happens
50. Some Of Us Are Sicker Than Others
51. We're All Here Because We're Not All There
52. Addiction Is An Equal Opportunity Destroyer
53. Gratitude Is The Attitude
54. H.A.L.T. = Don't Get Too Hungry, Angry, Lonely, or Tired
55. Another Friend Of Bill W's
56. God Is Never Late
57. Have A Good Day Unless You've Made Other Plans
58. Shit Happens
59. E.G.O. = Edging God Out
60. 90 Meetings 90 Days
61. You Are Not Alone
62. Wherever You Go, There You Are

63. Don't Drink, Read The Big Book, And Go To Meetings
64. Use The 24-Hour Plan
65. Make Use Of Telephone Therapy
66. Stay In Recovery For Yourself
67. Look For Similarities Rather Than Differences
68. Remember Your Last Drunk
69. Remember That Addiction Is Incurable, Progressive, And Fatal
70. Try Not To Place Conditions On Your Recovery
71. When All Else Fails Follow Directions
72. Count Your Blessings
73. Share Your Happiness
74. Respect The Anonymity O Others
75. Pain Is Optional
76. Let Go Of Old Ideas
77. Try To Replace Guilt With Gratitude
78. What Goes Around, Comes Around
79. Change Is A Process, Not An Event
80. Take The Cotton Out Of Your Ears And Put It In Your Mouth
81. Call Your Sponsor Before, Not After, You Take The First Drink
82. Sick And Tired Of Being Sick And Tired

83. It's The First Drink That Gets You Drunk
84. To Keep It, You Have To Give It Away
85. P.L.O.M. = Poor Little Old Me
86. Remember Happiness And Serenity Are An Inside Job
87. Any Addict Clean Is A Miracle
88. Take What You Can Use And Leave The Rest
89. We Demand Less And Give More
90. Believe In God Or Be God
91. If Only . . .
92. Help Is Only A Phone Call Away
93. Around The Program Or In The Program?
94. You Can't Give Away What You Don't Have
95. One Drink Is Too Many And A Thousand Not Enough
96. Welcome And "Keep Coming Back"
97. Anger Is But One Letter Away From Danger
98. Courage To Change . . .
99. Easy Does It, But Do It
100. Bring The Body And The Mind Will Follow

116. PRAYER OF ST. FRANCIS ASSISI

Lord, make me an instrument
of Your peace!
Where there is hatred, let me sow love.
Where there is injury, pardon.
Where there is doubt, faith.
Where there is despair, hope.
Where there is darkness, light.
Where there is sadness, joy.

O Divine Master,
Grant that I may not so much seek
To be consoled as to console.
To be understood as to understand.
To be loved as to love.
For it is in giving
that we receive.
It is in pardoning
that we are pardoned.
It is in dying
that we are born to eternal life.

117. SERENITY PRAYER

God grant me the serenity
To accept the things I cannot change;
The courage to change the things I can;
And the wisdom to know the difference.

Living one day at a time;
Enjoying one moment at a time;
Accepting hardship as the pathway to peace;

Taking, as He did,
This sinful world as it is,
Not as I would have it;
Trusting that He will
Make all things right
If I surrender to His Will;

That I may be
reasonably happy in this life,
And supremely happy with Him
Forever in the next.

118.   SANSKRIT PROVERB

Look to this day,
For it is life,
The very life of life.
In its brief course lies all
The realities and verities of existence,
The bliss of growth,
The splendor of action,
The glory of power.
For yesterday is but a dream,
And tomorrow is only a vision.
But today, well lived,
Makes every yesterday
A dream of happiness
And every tomorrow
A vision of hope.
Look well, therefore, to this day.

119.   TO BE PRAYER

O Lord, I ain't what I ought to be,
And I ain't what I want to be,
And I ain't what I'm going to be,
But O Lord, I thank You
That I ain't what I used to be.

THE TWELVE STEPS OF
ALCOHOLICS ANONYMOUS

1. We admitted we were powerless over alcohol—that our lives had become unmanageable.
2. Came to believe that a Power greater than ourselves could restore us to sanity.
3. Made a decision to turn our will and our lives over to the care of God *as we understood Him.*
4. Made a searching and fearless moral inventory of ourselves.
5. Admitted to God, to ourselves, and to another human being the exact nature of our wrongs.
6. Were entirely ready to have God remove all these defects of character.
7. Humbly asked Him to remove our shortcomings.
8. Made a list of all persons we had harmed, and became willing to make amends to them all.
9. Made direct amends to such people wherever possible, except when to do so would injure them or others.
10. Continued to take personal inventory and when we were wrong promptly admitted it.
11. Sought through prayer and meditation to improve our conscious contact with God *as we understood Him,* praying only for knowledge of His will for us and the power to carry that out.
12. Having had a spiritual awakening as the result of these steps, we tried to carry this message to alcoholics, and to practice these principles in all our affairs.

The Twelve Steps reprinted with permission of A.A. World Services, Inc., New York, New York.

HAZELDEN INFORMATION AND EDUCATIONAL SERVICES is a division of the Hazelden Foundation, a not-for-profit organization. Since 1949, Hazelden has been a leader in promoting the dignity and treatment of people afflicted with the disease of chemical dependency.

The mission of the foundation is to improve the quality of life for individuals, families, and communities by providing a national continuum of information, education, and recovery services that are widely accessible; to advance the field through research and training; and to improve our quality and effectiveness through continuous improvement and innovation.

Stemming from that, the mission of this division is to provide quality information and support to people wherever they may be in their personal journey—from education and early intervention, through treatment and recovery, to personal and spiritual growth.

Although our treatment programs do not necessarily use everything Hazelden publishes, our bibliotherapeutic materials support our mission and the Twelve Step philosophy upon which it is based. We encourage your comments and feedback.

The headquarters of the Hazelden Foundation are in Center City, Minnesota. Additional treatment facilities are located in Chicago, Illinois; New York, New York; Plymouth, Minnesota; St. Paul, Minnesota; and West Palm Beach, Florida. At these sites, we provide a continuum of care for men and women of all ages. Our Plymouth facility is designed specifically for youth and families.

For more information on Hazelden, please call **1-800-257-7800**. Or you may access our World Wide Web site on the Internet at **http://www.hazelden.org**.

HAZELDEN INFORMATION
AND
EDUCATIONAL SERVICES
P.O. Box 176
15251 Pleasant Valley Road
Center City, MN 55012-0176

HAZELDEN°

For price and order information, or a free catalog,
please call our Telephone Representatives.

1-800-328-9000
(Toll Free. U.S., Canada, and the Virgin Islands)

1-612-213-4000
(Outside the U.S., and Canada)

1-612-213-4590
(24-Hour FAX)

http://www.hazelden.org
(World Wide Web site on Internet)